Distraction

Being human in the digital age

A book by Mark Curtis

website www.futuretext.com

Copyright 2004 futuretext Limited
Issue Date 15 July 2005
Published by
futuretext
36 St George St
Mayfair
London
W1S 2FW
UK
Email:info@futuretext.com
www.futuretext.com

ISBN:0-9544327-4-6

Contents

Distraction: being human in the digital age

Preamble

Introduction

Part One: The Social Price of New Technology

Part Two: The Social Potential of New Technology

Preamble

"Distraction" has grown out of my work and observations over the last 10 years. It is about the very real day to day issues we face with communications technology and society, and as such contains much that is first person and subjective. It is not an academic piece of original research – instead I've drawn on a wide variety of sources to illustrate and inform. Included among these are personal anecdotes because I believe that stories are an entertaining way to communicate.

So much new emerges every week that I've started a web site to accompany this book – **www.distractionculture.com** – I'm adding stuff all the time, and it's also a place where you can send me feedback and comment.

Lots of people have helped me. Most of all my lovely daughters who provide endless insights (sometimes deliberately, often without intending to) – it's a cliché but if you want to known about adult society tomorrow watch today's teenagers. Much of the content of this book has been developed with Mike Beeston and Olof Schybergson (thanks for the cover!) with whom I work at Fjord (**www.fjord.co.uk**), They are thoughtful and inspiring experts. Then there are many others I have worked with over the last few years, at Razorfish, Fjord, and client companies who have freely given support, feedback or vigorous debate. Amongst them in no particular order are Andrew Curry, Jo Rabin, Celia Romaniuk (especially for the constant flow of input), Steve Graham, Lauren Walter, Iain Perring, Peter Seidler, Tucker Viemeister, Paul Wielgus, Ajit Jaokar, Bonnie Baker, Tomi Ahonen, Molly Wright Steenson, Dave Cook, Glenn Cornett, Peter Cowie aka Top Banana, Sappho Clissit, Hugo Drayton, Christian Lindholm, Kate and Shane Ginsberg, Matt Woolf. Thanks to Neil Crofts who made me realise you can get published and is annoyingly challenging all the time.

This book is dedicated with love to Cherry, an expert on distraction.
Thank you for your wisdom. Please distract me forever.

DISTRACTION
Digital culture and how it's changing our world

Introduction

I make my living by knowing about digital communications. Specifically by understanding how organisations – usually companies – should use new technology to communicate with their customers. By digital I mean the things people usually mean: the Internet, digital TV, mobile phones (even though not all of these are always strictly digital). Until recently I found this enormously exciting. It seemed to me to be a reasonably "grown-up" way of earning a crust and beyond that I enjoyed the sense of being at the edge of something unformed and nascent.

I'm not so sure any more.

10 years ago I read a feature in the Economist that changed my life. I am uncomfortably aware that this statement endorses that publication's claim to give you the advantage over your rivals of better knowledge, but in this case it is true.

The article highlighted the issue of **convergence**, a good term now out of fashion. In this context convergence was the coming together of computing, TV and telephony to create new communications and business opportunities.

I spotted one. And together with a part time sheep farmer who had previously been an advertising executive, we set up a company to help build the communications output of this brave new world. We struggled even to know what to call it: few used the term digital at that time. We settled on interactive media after laborious attempts to define what we meant by it (the difference was that the user could talk back to the medium we decided). Others called it new media – and still do. After some bold and impossibly ambitious experiments with "interactive" and networked (they could talk to each other) kiosks in pubs, CD Roms and a gay bulletin board, by 1995 it was clear the action was going to be centred around the World Wide Web, and accordingly we began to focus on helping companies build web sites.

The first client we approached took us for lunch in a pub. He was and is a very experienced buyer of media space. Over a pint or three we told him what we saw in the future. Correctly he identified that we were a couple of arrogant young men who were trying to tell him that if he did not listen, he would be out of a job in five years time. He sent us away with a flea in our ear.

Three months later the phone rang. It was the media buyer. He'd been reading and hearing things that made him suspect we might after all be worth talking to. We never looked back (and remain indebted to Patrick Burton, Paul Wielgus and Ali Jarvis of Allied Domecq for believing at least part of what we said). We went on to work with the FT, RAC, Nat West, Virgin, BP and many others.

In 1998 we sold the company we had started to a New York outfit called Razorfish, run by two charismatic Minnesotans – Jeff Dachis and Craig Kanarick – who were intent on digital world domination. We joined in the ride and it was as memorable as they promised. But by the summer of 2000 it was clear that the famous Internet Bubble had burst. Razorfish was a supplier of Internet services and suddenly no-one wanted to buy. The company declined faster than anyone knew how to spell out redundancy, and it was a very sad time.

As the web winter set in, the doom sayers emerged gleefully from the forests of doubt where they had been lurking impatiently. They had of course seen this coming all along and now we could all gratefully forget about this digital nonsense and return to wearing suits. I remember reading an article about the new managing director of the London office of a web services company where he actually said this (the bit about the suits). Hurray the madness was over.

And it had been mad. But I'm not going to dissect that here. My issue is that the perception which took hold, and to some extent is still at large, was that this "digital" thing was going away, had never had any real meaning and that its impact was superficial at best.

This is a very dangerous fallacy.

Digital technology – essentially the bit that deals with communications – is changing our world more than most people remotely imagine. This book is about that change. Parts of it could possibly have been written three or even five years ago. However the outlines of the impact of mobile technology are beginning to slope out from the mist and affect the story for better or worse. It is time to give it some narrative form and see if it makes sense.

Our world is changing shape. This should not be a surprise as it has happened before. I do not of course mean something as dramatic as a shift from being a sphere to a cube. In this book, I am more interested in the way we think of our universe. If you define reality as that which we think we experience, then history is well furnished with examples of man's perceptions of the world around him changing fundamentally.

These are very important moments though at the time they happen, it is hard to see what the effect will be.

You'd have to go back to the sixties for another decade when our world has

Mark Curtis

changed (the pill, pop music, drugs, the moon landing) so much as in the last ten years. The changes we are living through now are perhaps less raucous and demanding of our attention as sexual freedom or the rise of the teenager. That does not mean they are less important. In the long term, they may be more so.

This re-shaping of our landscape is happening at the same time as a tremendous shift in the way we structure our social networks, caused and enabled largely by new technology. The world of our friends and acquaintances is mediated increasingly by electronic address books – in sim cards, mail browsers and buddy lists (the address books used by instant messenger services such as MSN Messenger). Are these going to support or disrupt the traditional social networks – or is this an artificial distinction suggesting that there is nothing to worry about?

We do know that social capital – the store of goodwill that helps us have easier relationships with people – is in decline. Will digital halt this or change its course?

We cannot take for granted that all progress is good, as the Victorians did. In "Why Things Bite Back[1]" Edward Tenner developed a compelling theory that every technological advance carries with it what he called a "revenge" effect, a kind of unintended consequence. Frequently this is chronic and long term, by which he meant low level and hard to detect, but often much harder to deal with than the problem that was being addressed in the first place. For example pesticides eliminate pests, but damage other parts of the food chain too, which in time makes the growing of crops harder because natural predators of other pests are affected for the worse. Indeed the original target pests themselves often out evolve the poison, and the new superbugs are much harder to get rid of.

The digital revolution, now roughly ten years old, will not be without its revenge effects, most of which will be social. This book begins to examine what some of these might be and suggests how we can ameliorate their influence and build on some of the very positive aspects of new technology.

A word on terminology: I use the phrases 'digital communications', 'new media', 'new technology' (and probably others) interchangeably. By them I mean to describe the new types of technology we use to communicate with each other and with machines: the Internet, e-mail, mobile voice telephony, SMS, Instant Messaging, web sites. I also include digital TV and radio, as increasingly these are interactive and cannot be seen in splendid isolation.

This is not an academic treatise. The book is informed by three things: ten years work developing digital communication, observations I make on what I see around me in everyday life and the stories that I hear, and lastly the books and articles I have read in my own struggle to understand what is going on. Many of these are fascinating but rarely see the light of day beyond a narrow audience of those intimately

---

[1] Fourth Estate, 1996

bound up with this (still new and evolving) world. I have tried to write for a broad audience: people who have seen this new technology enter their lives and are trying to make sense of it. Someone asked me if it was a handbook for the digital age: that would certainly be an overly ambitious claim, but it is intended as a guide of sorts.

The book has two halves: in part one – The Social Price of New Technology – chapters one to seven examine the impact of new communications on society. In the second half – The Social Potential of New Technology – it explores what opportunities we can grasp to make our lives better.

We start by looking at the unfortunate tendency of the digital era to strip out context. An essential problem with the digitisation of things is that context has a tendency to go awol and subtleties of meaning and connection are lost. I'll give examples of this and explore why it happens, if it is important and what could be done about it. Context gives meaning, reward, focus, helps us make decisions. In the age of 10,000 songs in your pocket, why are sales of old fashioned records booming? Yet we run the risk of believing that data is everything, and confusing information with knowledge.

We then look at how our sense of time and space may be changing radically, and not for the first time in human history. Digital space is upon us but what will it look like?

The importance of this question now becomes apparent when we consider that the widespread adoption of mobile technology over the last five years is a social tipping point of no return: for we are becoming 'always on'. Not only connected to the network, but distributing ourselves through it. Mobile opens up radical new communications possibilities still barely tapped. Expect before too long to see graffiti sprayed in thin air, messages you view through a phone, like invisible sticky post-its in all kinds of unexpected places.

The risk is that this is all just used as a distraction. Is it possible for individual humans to deal elegantly with the abundant communication possibilities of the modern world? There is a plenty of evidence that we are in real danger of paying more attention to the potential of a text message than the here and now around us. Looking at our emerging behaviour as we seek to find ways to incorporate e-mail and mobile into our lives, it is clear that the boundaries between private and public space are breaking down. Perhaps it is not so much the famous 'death of distance' that we are witnessing, but a near-fatal wounding of closeness.

At this stage it is worth asking a question – can media have a distracting effect? Is their influence overrated? We look at dramatic evidence from the most powerful country in the world, and one of the smallest, that television alone has changed societies, and not always for the better. Now we are adding many more channels of all kinds to our lives.

In fact, communication may just be reaching the stage where we cannot deal

Mark Curtis

with the volume, and some kind of radical response will be required at all levels of society simply to cope. Spam is an early warning signal: surprisingly it appears that organizations are having just as many problems with sustainable communication as private citizens. We are also destabilized by some of the uses we put the technology to: current social norms may not be able deal with the explosion of dating, flirting and sex made so easily available.

These are good examples of how we use new communications possibilities to feed the culture of immediacy that pervades Western life. We want gratification now. However at this point the revenge effect steps in with a vengeance: in feeding the short term pleasure principle, new technology often ends up making life more complicated. Lack of time is the most frequent complaint of harassed adults in the early 21st century, but we are working no more hours per week than previous generations. So where has all the time gone? We look at how a simple act like buying and using a digital camera can eat up time unexpectedly in consumption work.

So what can we do to make the best of new technology? Firstly I argue that it is time to push the new media and make them work better for us: I suggest guidelines and challenges for improving the quality of what we use and consume. These include a call for greater story telling and beauty in these often very functional environments. We have to drag context back to the surface from where it is too often hidden in the depths, and explore how we can invigorate digital conversation with body language.

Next we examine how our sense of self, maybe the most precious thing we have, is changing and how technology can both threaten this and be used to build it up. What can we learn from a virtual hotel run by teenagers? Digital gives us an opportunity to map out and fashion new expressions of identity. New kinds of trust will be required, and at the same time, privacy may become a thing of the past but we will be prepared to trade it for security.

Digital connects us together more than ever before. We have only just started to explore the ramifications of this. New thinking in science, partly catalysed by questions about how the Internet works, shows that networks underpin much of the way the universe works. We can and should embrace the wonderful ability of communications to build and reinforce new social networks and structures in order to reach towards a more interdependent world.

At the same time we look at how we need to change many of our habits, and take control not of the technology (not usually the problem), but of ourselves. Only by doing so can we hope to fight off distraction and build long lasting value in society. Indeed we could do with a new determination to construct for the future, to think long term.

Perhaps we can do this first at a personal level: for the final hopeful sign of digital technology is that it is enabling normal people to find new levels of creativity for themselves. We are all going to become media owners, in the process reducing our reliance on traditional content suppliers and evolving more multi-faceted identities. We will also leave a clearer sense of the complex beings we are for our children's children. If we can use new technology to be creative and celebrate us, we can leave a vibrant legacy for the future.

Erik Davis in Techgnosis relates the following story, taken in turn from Plato, and narrated by Socrates. It concerns Thoth, the Egyptian god of magic and invention. "...One day Thoth approached King Thamus with an offer of a brand new *techne* (art): writing. By giving the gift of writing to the king, Thoth hoped to pass on its wonders to all of the Egyptian people, and he promised Thamus that the new invention would not only augment memory, but amplify wisdom as well. Thamus carefully considered the matter, weighing the pros and cons of this major communications upgrade. Finally the king rejected the gift, saying that his people would be better off with out the new device. And reading between the lines of the story, it's clear that Socrates and Plato agree."

Thamus feared that the gift of writing would take away his people's memory. He reasoned that once you could write ideas and stories down, the facility to remember them would fade. As Davis points out, it is hard to disagree when you consider the loss of oral tradition in societies that have put pen to paper and ink to press.

Well, Thoth has been laying on the gifts thickly recently, and we have no all-powerful Thamus to say no thank you. As media guru Marshall McLuhan observed (some time ago now), when you gain from technology, you always lose something too. The aim of this book is to contribute to the debate about losses and gains in the field of human communication.

Mark Curtis

PART ONE
The Social Price
Of New Technology

PART ONE
The Social Price Of New Technology

Chapter One
The Decline of Context

This chapter argues that digital technology often impoverishes the very content it is so good at distributing, by reducing the amount of context available to us to make sense of what we see and hear. When the bits around the edges get lost, often for reasons of technological efficiency, we lose understanding too. Machine delivered data still cannot always replicate what humans know.

Only Connect

In a cupboard at home I have a treasured collection of 45 rpm, 7 inch vinyl singles. Each one carries memories. Some still have their original covers, creased, faded and worn. A few have my name inked across them in an adolescent scrawl. I did this in a vain attempt to retain them at parties – though many disappeared. I lost all my T-Rex and Slade singles before the 70's were over (if anyone reading knows where they are, could you please return them?) Those that survived beery teenage nights carry reminders etched onto the music itself in the form of scratches and grooves unrecorded by the bands.

Music is particularly good at evoking memories. It can be very closely tied to important moments in our life. Radio DJ Simon Bates made a kitsch and much parodied feature out of "Our Tune", where listeners wrote in with their personal story and a particular song that was sometimes the backdrop, occasionally a lead actor in the drama. It usually made for saccharine listening, but the idea touched a nerve because we can all relate to it.

Damaged vinyl is extremely annoying, and its propensity to scratch was a very good reason to embrace CD's when they came along – as most people did. But – at the risk of sounding like a nostalgic 40 something – there is a physical quality to vinyl in a sleeve that CD's have never matched. Anyone who bought them will remember the sticky quality that a single or album had when you first slid them out of the sleeve – caused I think by static. Mentioning this to a colleague, he went into a reverie: "smooth and black like a bowling ball that's been polished" he enthused. It signalled a sense of newness, that this music had not been touched by anyone. The smell of acetate added to the sensual impression. And, especially on albums, there was plenty of room for design to tell you more about what was on the inside. Even the label communicated: in 1977 anything from Stiff Records came with the familiar hand drawn black and white logo and the promise of musical eccentricity that Stiff embodied (The Blockheads, Wreckless Eric, Elvis Costello). In fact labels could even be a good primitive search system – rifling rapidly through a rack of records anything with a deep gold label signalled Sire, and in my collection that meant the Ramones.

Sights, smells, touch – these are context for the sounds. But when music goes digital, we lose all of it, except the memories, and even these are lessened by the loss of contextual prompts – be they a label, sleeve or irritating scratch. Apple's iPod is advertised as the portable device which can hold up to "10,000 songs". With an iPod you can carry the equivalent of 700 or more albums everywhere, listen to them on the move or plug into the nearest Hi-fi and inflict your taste on everyone. (This is already happening at parties: teenagers turning up armed with their Pods and arguing over who gets jacked in). You can create your own "playlists" for whatever mood or occasion in seconds. In the digital world, you can swap music easily with others, even if it is illegal.

In 2004 when it hit the mainstream, Apple advertisements showed blacked-out silhouette figures dancing to the sounds from their iPod – nothing else existed in their world but the music. Look at an MP3 file on your computer – it reveals itself as a standard icon, sometimes with the name of the track (but not the artist), sometimes without even that, just a number. Of course the content is still there and just as good to listen to (though some would dispute that, claiming that vinyl delivers a warmer sound).

Of course it is utterly wrong to say that content MUST have context to be worthwhile. Some viral humour – the kind you get on e-mail – is very funny and no-one cares who wrote it, where it has been. Arguably, where music is concerned, lack of distracting reference points may allow the listener to enjoy the content without prejudice. If I don't know the band wear Stetsons and spurs, I may just give country music a chance.

Such a purist point of view ignores the contribution to overall enjoyment that context brings with it. A record or even CD just is a more interesting and revealing artefact than an MP3, even with the same musical content[2]. Deep down the latter

---

[2] Though I know people who dispute this. Perhaps it is the physicality of the record that lends it some intangible extra, perhaps also that an MP3 is still very limited in the information it carries, whereas a record tends to have much more.

Mark Curtis

is just a string of zeroes and ones, which when decoded cause speakers to vibrate in a way that closely resembles the artist's intention. The reduction of everything to strings of digits is at the heart of the issue. It is a property of digital that it has *an inherent tendency to strip out context* wherever it can. Why is this?

Compression and decay, precision and reproduction

One set of reasons lie around bandwidth and capacity. There is a finite amount of storage space on devices – that is PC's, storage media (zip drives, CD's, smartmedia etc). Bandwidth, which is the capacity of wired or wireless connections to stream data from one place to another at any given moment, has also usually been scarce compared to demand. A bit like the M25 motorway, whenever another lane is added, we invent ways to fill it.

The answer has been compression technology. This takes the strings of zeroes and ones, and cuts out the unwanted bits which make no difference to your enjoyment of the content when you come to consume it. Again no argument that it's a great invention which allows huge quantities of stuff to be digitised, copied and distributed at speed.

The second bundle of reasons is that digital things tend to remain precisely what they are and no more. Time and place have almost no effect on them. They pick up little on their travels across networks, do not decay, are not smelly – in short are differentiated from the outside usually by file names or numbers. The result is that at its worst, which is the norm, digital content lacks charm, magic and depth. In fact digital things usually only appeal to one or at best two senses, constrained as they are by the ability of technology (so far) to replicate taste, touch and smell.

Thirdly the digital world, at least in theory, allows a very high degree of precision for locating things. A web site address takes you straight to the place you wish to be. If you don't know it, you can Google it. OK – so search engines don't always deliver terrific results, but considering the scale of the challenge they are remarkably accurate. Today Google claims that it searches 8,058,044,651 web pages. I'm glad not to be doing this in an archive of 8 billion sheets of paper. Additionally the technology allows users to create precise pointers to things in lots of ways. On your PC you can do this with the command 'Create Shortcut', or for a Mac user 'Make Alias'. Web links are pointers. So are the telephone numbers stored in your phone's address book. Paradoxically digital both de-emphasises context and makes it easier to connect to other things.

Lastly, digital technology makes it very easy to copy things, because all the technology has to do is to replicate the content (zeroes and ones) exactly. This has lots of effects. It is a nightmare for the music and film industries with which they are still grappling. The flip side is that it has fuelled the phenomenon known as peer to peer file sharing. It allows anyone with a PC to cut and paste, and they do. An interesting news item can be shared with friends and colleagues in ten or so key strokes and mouse clicks. (Frequently it loses the context of the web site from which it was taken, even though it may be useful to have the context that an article comes from a trusted source, for example, the BBC.) Many content web sites have embraced this issue by adding the functionality to allow users to send their content to others – usually it's a link. Of course they have done this as a form of viral marketing for their wares, and a link, if pursued, takes the user to the source where at least the context is fuller. In addition, because a digital copy is always identical to the original, digital artefacts rarely feel unique.

At this stage I'd like to emphasise that I have used the words *tendency* and *tend* deliberately. I recognise that digital *can* add context if it is asked to do so. For instance a digital camera will (if it's owner has set the clock function) know what time and day a picture was taken. Theoretically a cameraphone will even know where it was taken. This is certainly contextual information (often tediously called "metadata") of rich value. I'm going to argue later that we should be designing much greater use of this into digital systems.

Why is context important?

Context helps give **meaning**. You can hear Fulsom City Blues by Johnny Cash, and enjoy it for its sound, alone. But you are definitely missing something if you do not know that it was recorded in the eponymous Fulsom Prison, and that the crowd cheering when Johnny sings "I shot a man in Reno just to watch him die" are convicts. This kind of information comes in sleeve notes or by verbal anecdote, but not on MP3s (not yet anyway).

In the church of Santa Maria Novella in Florence is a picture of the Holy Trinity by Masaccio. It is in itself a remarkable work which furthered the science of painting in perspective championed by Giotto the century before. You may know about it before you go, but nothing prepares you for the reality in situ. Painted on a wall within the church, the artist has conjured up the illusion that you are looking into a chapel which is part of the architectural structure of the building you are in. The trick is completed by the (painted) tomb which connects the bottom of the picture to the floor of the church itself. It is important to be there to appreciate the full effect, because Masaccio intended this to be seen in the context both of a place of worship and an architectural setting. You can find a photograph of the Holy Trinity on the web, but not truly see it as it was meant to be seen.

In The Social Life of Information[3], authors John Seely Brown and Paul Duguid

---

[3] HBS Press, 2004

Mark Curtis

describe a research trip one of them made to Portugal. In an old archive he had to read correspondence from the 1700's. The dust raised by opening each of the old letters triggered asthma attacks. One day a fellow historian came in and to his aston-ishment pored over another box of letters in a very unusual way.

"He read barely a word. Instead, he picked out bundles of letters and, in a move that sent my sinuses into shock, ran each letter beneath his nose and took a deep breath, at times almost inhaling the letter itself but always getting a good dose of dust. Sometimes, after a particularly profound sniff, he would open the letter, glance at it briefly, make a note and move on.

Choking behind my mask, I asked him what he was doing. He was he told me, a medieval historian (a profession to avoid if you have asthma). He was documenting outbreaks of cholera. When that disease occurred in a town in the eighteenth cen-tury, all letters from that town were disinfected with vinegar to prevent the disease from spreading. By sniffing for faint traces of vinegar that survived 250 years and noting the date and source of the letters, he was able to chart the progress of cholera outbreaks." I've yet to come across the e-mail I could smell.

If it carries personal meaning, then context may also deliver an emotional **re-ward**, often in the form of memories. A battered old diary can be reproduced digit-ally – especially if it is just writing or text – but it is hard to reproduce digitally the feeling that one can get from the whole item in your hands. In my wallet I have a dog-eared old ticket for the Empire State Building which dates from my first visit ever to New York. Of course I could get a new one on my next visit, but it wouldn't be the same.

Context can bring things into **focus**, and add to our understanding of the whole. A few miles outside Dorchester in Dorset, lies one of the most important historical sites in England – Maiden Castle. It is not the typical stone built ruin associated with the word castle. Maiden is pre-Roman, dating back possibly to 3000BC. It domi-nates, in fact is, an entire hill. The structure now contains no wood (rotted long ago) and what stone remains, is visible only at the top. Chiefly it consists of concentric rings of ditch and embankment on a massive scale. It is the largest Iron Age hill fort in Europe. I had seen aerial photographs on the web before visiting which gave a good impression. However only the walk up from the road and along the entire circumference of the outer defensive ring really tells you how big this is. It takes a whole hour to go right round. There just isn't an alternative if you wish to appreciate the scale of the fortifications, or speculate on how many people could have lived here, or what it was like when it finally fell to Roman assault.

Context can help us make **decisions** too. Faced with a choice between previ-ously unknown retailers selling me things on the web, I can only choose based on what I see through the screen of my computer. In the physical world, there are plenty of other contextual clues to use. In this shop do the assistants smile? In that one does the food smell good? Is it in a good neighbourhood? Are there plenty of other customers? Do they look happy or aggrieved? Some of these, with care, can be established through the web[4] – but usually such pointers are left out because few think to design them in.

Design and context are inextricably linked. The world we live in is becoming more and more designed every year. It has been an inevitable human response to the rise of complexity. Of course design, of sorts, has existed throughout history. A brief look at any collection of late medieval armour tells the story of people concerned with both functionality and aesthetics, who hired expert designers. However 21st century men and women are faced with a legion of challenges which would have been totally unfamiliar to our ancestors. Design is needed to give guidance if you are navigating an airport, driving a car, using a computer or mobile phone or microwave, constructing flatpack furniture. When it fails, as it often does in the latter case, life can briefly become miserable. Often this happens because of over reliance on the power of information.

Information Blindness

Information has been raised to an almost Olympian status in our society – it rules the world[5]. According to one technology guru information "is becoming the commodity of...most value[6]". The digital revolution is both powered and measured by the ability to transmit, process and store information. PC's become out of date within two years of manufacture because under the famous Moore's Law, the power of chips to process information roughly doubles every 18 months. Mobile phone operators continuously plan to upgrade their networks in order to build capacity – for data or information. We live apparently in the "Information Age". IT is of course *Information* Technology.

According to research published in November 2003 by the University of California[7], more "information" has been created and stored in the last five years than at any time before in human history. In 2002 print, film, magnetic and optical storage media produced about five exabytes of new information. Five exabytes of information is the equivalent of 1/2 million new libraries the size of the print section of the US Library of Congress, which is America's library of record. They believe

---

[4] eBay has created an outstanding system for creating context around buyers or sellers where they simply rate each other. This is one way in which digital technology has created a solution which is an improvement on what we had before.

[5] Though most people would probably claim that it is of low value to them

[6] Danny Hillis quoted in "What's Next?" Wiley, 2002

[7] http://www.sims.berkeley.edu/research/projects/how-much-info-2003/

Mark Curtis

that at the current rate 800MB of information is produced for each member of the human race each year. That would take 30 feet of books to store. Remember this is *new* information. It is already double what was happening three years ago. Most of it is digital – 92% is stored on magnetic media such as hard drives.

Where is this coming from? It surely cannot be that in such a short space of time the human race has trebled its productivity (of information). There are two sources – ourselves and the infrastructure we have created to distribute and record data activity. To take a simple example: every time an executive cc's an e-mail, more data is created. Not only on his PC, but on his e-mail server too, on everyone else's PCs and servers, and all the back-ups too. Is it pollution? It's certainly waste. Everytime you make a mobile phone call, the details are saved – and not just to bill you. The data could be as simple as time and length of call, and to whom it was made. To that can be added (depending on the system and your government) where you made the call, from what kind of handset and the contents of the call too. All this is stored somewhere. 10 years ago instant messaging, e-mail, SMS, web sites – these all barely existed. Now we are getting into our stride in using them, small wonder that we are seeing such an accelerated rise in the volume of data.

But a blind belief that data in itself is going to solve problems is misplaced. The availability of data in itself does not guarantee anything. It is what we do with it. Google is a clever search engine but frequently returns results which are meaningless. The failure to distinguish between data that means something and data that is useless has led to a great deal of waste in corporate spending on IT systems in the last ten years, especially in the fashionable field of Knowledge Management.

The theory sounds good: together we (the company) know a lot more than we can easily get our hands on. It's a hidden asset and we need to unlock the power of that knowledge. Look! Lots of it is now there in data form because we communicate so much electronically and store all of it! So all we have to do is figure out a way of storing and navigating all that information in order to find the golden egg laying goose.

The theory however has a flaw: it is too focussed on IT and not enough on what people actually do. Data is different from knowledge. The latter is something that people have. Call it "know how", and remember that "know that" is something different. Sometimes these are called explicit and tacit knowledge. Explicit, know *that* knowledge can indeed be captured as data and often is. Tacit or know *how* knowledge is the total of experiences that a human has around an issue which is much harder to write down or capture, but nevertheless informs our actions and makes us experts. You can buy all the baby care books in the world but nothing prepares you for the experience of parenthood, and over time the tacit knowledge you build up of your child is much more valuable than the manuals, and hard to capture digitally.

Seely Brown and Duguid are especially insightful about this. "First, knowledge usually entails a knower. That is, where people treat information as independent and more-or-less self-sufficient, they seem more inclined to associate knowledge with someone. In general, it sounds right to ask, "Where is that information?" but odd to ask, "Where's that knowledge?" as if knowledge normally lay around waiting to be picked up. It seems more reasonable to ask, "Who knows that?".

Second, given this personal attachment, knowledge appears harder to detach than information. People treat information as a self-contained substance. It is something that people pick up, possess, pass around, put in a database, lose, find, write down, accumulate, count, compare, and so forth. Knowledge, by contrast, doesn't take so kindly to ideas of shipping, receiving, and quantification. It is hard to pick up and hard to transfer. You might expect someone to send you or point you to the information they have, but not to the knowledge they have.

Third, one reason knowledge may be so hard to give and receive is that knowledge seems to require more by way of assimilation. Knowledge is something we digest rather than merely hold."

No wonder so many knowledge management initiatives have struggled to succeed. They simply do not take account of context and the human factor. Incidentally the blind belief that more data is a solution for everything is also visible in the way software manufacturers provide increasingly complex help directories and search engines, and in some cases even feature "help about help" where the hapless user goes to discover how to use the help section. One of the best mobile phone designers I know makes it a mantra that a phone should never need a help system: if it does, it has been poorly designed.

A wise colleague, Paul Wielgus, once taught me that when, for instance, a politician speaks, there are three ways in which humans evaluate him or her, logos, pathos and ethos. Logos are the actual words you use – the data if you like. Pathos is the degree to which the audience empathises with the speaker – how warm or like us they seem. Ethos is the degree to which they seem to really believe in what they are saying and have integrity. When we hear someone speak, at say a public event, we tend to form opinions about them much more for their ethos and pathos more than the words they use. In other words, the information they reveal is less powerful than they way they present it.

However, much of our digital world is powered and measured by the ability to transmit, process and store information. The punter who walks into Dixons to buy a PC may not have heard of Moore's Law (the number of transistors per square inch on integrated circuits will double every year for the foreseeable future), or Metcalfe's Law (the value of a network is proportional to the square of the number of people using it), but they will know that technology becomes obsolescent pretty fast these days. Likely as not, they'll specify what they want by clock speed, memory and disk space. If they are buying a phone, they may consider the promise of 3G and know that beyond video it means a bigger, fatter connection.

The mosaic of meaning is all around us, woven into the fabric of life. At worst, new technology knocks colourful parts out of the picture. At best, it can add new tiles, but never replace all perspectives of experience. What if digital was also profoundly to affect our sense of perspective?

PART ONE
The Social Price Of New Technology

CHAPTER TWO
Space Matters

Twice in Western civilisation we have substantially changed the way we think about time and space. New dimensions were radically introduced to our concept of the universe in the Renaissance, and again at the beginning of the 20th century. Both times the new thinking was visible not only in science but also in art. Now another shift of the same kind is taking place. It will alter the way we relate to each other and the world around us. This chapter tracks the history of these events to show how important they are, and suggests that the new world of communications is bringing infinity closer to us than we may have yet guessed.

It is now very hard to deny that the Internet and mobile phones have changed our lives. To support a statement like that, it's easy to focus on the superficial changes to the day to day pattern of our existence. For every human affected it will be different – the convenience of on-line transport timetables, the swiftness and insistence of texting, finding and sharing new music on-line, keeping a track on errant teenage offspring.

However a much deeper seismic shift is taking place, with long term implications that go well beyond adjustments to our daily rituals. Digital technology is reshaping the landscape of our imagination and reality. We are willing co-perpetrators of this shift.

The language of the new media points us in this direction. Cyberspace (a term probably coined by novelist William Gibson – of whom more in a moment), Virtual Reality, the World Wide Web – all these terms pre-figure the creation of something with epic scale. Books with titles like The Death of Distance and Warp Speed Branding point in the same direction. The new technology is changing our understanding of space and time.

It is hard to stress how important this is: such changes utterly transform how we see ourselves and the world around us. This in turn profoundly affects the way we behave.

Heaven is Above, Hell Below

This is not the first time in human history that this has happened. In a brilliant and intriguingly titled book – the Pearly Gates of Cyberspace[8] – Margaret Wertheim explores the history of mankind's conception of space. I make no apology for drawing from it heavily as her insights are riveting.

Wertheim begins her story in the middle ages in Western Europe. In the medieval worldview physical space was strictly limited. Beyond it was a spiritual space – heaven. The Italian poet Dante laid out the map of these spaces with precision in the Divine Comedy. He and his guide, the poet Virgil, go on a journey of exploration. Heaven, Purgatory (an anteroom for heaven), the world we live in and hell exist in two dimensions in this journey. Souls either go up to heaven, or down to hell. In each they find their places exactly – there are for instance nine circles of hell with chambers reserved specifically for each type of wrongdoer – procurers and seducers, flatterers, hypocrites, scandalmongers, traitors to guests and futurologists among them.

The medieval difficulty with space, as we understand it, goes back to Aristotle, who believed in a "full" universe. For Aristotle, because nature abhors a vacuum, space could not exist because nature would not let it. This is not easy for modern minds to grasp – after all what is it between me and the bloke next to me if not space? But it permeated western Christian thought to the extent that artists could not paint properly in three dimensions. They could represent *objects* realistically but not the space or area *in between* things. This is demonstrably seen in numerous illustrated manuscripts, the famous Wilton Diptych at the National Gallery, London or the Bayeux Tapestry.

However it did leave room for heaven: according to Wertheim "precisely because the medieval cosmos was limited to an extent, this vision of reality could also accommodate other kinds of space".

The first blows to this two dimensional edifice were administered bv artists, ironically working in the same part of the world – the city states of Northern Italy – as Dante did.

Giotto lead the revolution. According to Michael Levey[9] Giotto was regarded by his Florentine contemporaries as the man "who had changed the old "Greek" manner of painting into a modern one". In works such as the Arena Chapel in Padua he introduced a much more careful examination of the real physical world, twinned with considered representation. Comparing pictures by him and an earlier master, Levey notes that "where Cimabue's figures rise one above the other, seeming to oc-

---

[8] Virago, 1999
[9] "From Giotto to Cezanne, A Concise History of Painting"

Mark Curtis

cupy no more space than a handful of playing cards, Giotto's recede in depth. The eye senses weight in the shapes of the foreground kneeling angels, and space as existing between them and the enthroned Madonna."

Giotto was not wholly successful in his attempt to present a unified space. Buildings are different sizes and frequently viewed from alternative perspectives. Only later in the renaissance did painters such as Masaccio and Uccello give us a "continuous, homogenous, three-dimensional space" and "their new naturalistic artistic style helped to precipitate a revolution in thinking that would eventually demolish the great dualistic medieval cosmos, and would set western humanity within a new spatial scheme"(Wertheim). In other words, artists enabled mankind to view the world differently.

Consequently this was not just an artistic movement – the fashion for empirical observation or intense scrutiny affected, and then became the hall mark of, philosophy and science over the next couple of hundred years. Already in 1264, English scientist Roger Bacon had argued, in a treatise sent to Pope Clement IV, that the realistic use of geometry in art might be a powerful way to reveal to ordinary mortals the glories and truth of the scriptures. His view was that science could serve faith. However it fell out otherwise.

The roving eye

The interplay between art and science, cause and effect, is not necessarily a consecutive one-came-before-the-other sort of affair. Over mankind's history it is much more a continuous symbiotic process with spikes of activity and achievement. Initially the approach taken by artists to perspective suggested one central point of view (the centre of the picture) was the correct view. Gradually artists began to experiment with different viewpoints. This had the effect of freeing up the eye; in effect disembodying it, a move that reinforced the idea of a space in which the eye, and thus our imagination, could rove around. Influenced by the aesthetics of contemporary painters, Copernicus (1473 – 1543) saw that space was organised radically differently from the prevailing understanding. Other thinkers were intimately involved in this development – notably Galileo, Nicholas of Cusa and Johannes Kepler, but his name is the one linked to the massive shift in spatial understanding – the Copernican Revolution. He was the first to put forward the hypothesis that the earth moved round the sun. Initially he was not taken seriously – Martin Luther ranted that "this fool wishes to reverse the entire science of astronomy, but sacred scripture tells us that Joshua commanded the sun to stand still, and not the earth".

In the 17th century Galileo, using a new invention – the telescope – confirmed the theory, and much more. He established that celestial bodies were not perfect spheres, that there were thousands of previously unobserved stars and that space was just like that already implicitly envisioned by painters, a "vast, featureless, three dimensional void". The tight bonds between art and science are evident: Galileo knew all about perspective and had applied for a position to teach it at an academy in Florence. The poet John Milton met Galileo shortly before his death, and referred to him as the "Tuscan artist" viewing the moon "through optic glass" in Paradise Lost.

By this stage it is already possible to observe the inevitable process by which science was killing off the heavens. As Wertheim says "you cannot have it both ways: either the celestial realm is a metaphor for the spiritual space of heaven, a space populated by "angels," or it is a physical space filled with material planets inhabited by "aliens"."

The church saw this clearly; in 1632 after publishing "Dialogue on the Two Chief World Systems" Galileo was hauled in front of the Inquisition and at the age of 70 and under threat of torture, made in his own signed words to "abandon the false opinion the Sun is the centre of the world and immovable and that the Earth in not the centre of the world and moves".

No room for the angels

Within a few years however Isaac Newton began to hammer in the nails. He completed the revolution in scientific thinking that had been coming since Bacon. His theory of gravity explained not only how apples fell, but also how we did not fall off the earth, and that planets revolved around the sun. Gravity implied mass, and thus matter. "Matter now reigned supreme, not just on earth but throughout the cosmos…celestial space and terrestrial space were now united as one continuous physical domain" writes Wertheim. However "it is important to note here that this is a specifically Western problem. The reason we lost our spiritual space, as it were, is because we had linked it to celestial space. We had "located" it metaphorically speaking, up there beyond the stars. When celestial space became infinite, our spiritual space was thereby annihilated." Not all cultures have located their space likewise, which may explain some of the threat that the West seems to pose to Islam, and some of the attraction that Buddhism has for modern Westerners in search of soul space.

This book is not intended to be a thorough or continuous narrative of Western thinking – so now we have to skip forward to the start of the twentieth century, when once again art and science perform their mutual dance to the music of time. It is remarkable and surely not coincidental that the most momentous changes for three hundred years in artistic rendition and the scientific theory of space took place more or less simultaneously.

Let's take science first. Newton's cosmology had no creation story (he himself, deeply religious, would have been horrified by such a thought) – yet the question was inevitable – where had the universe come from? Einstein's General Theory of Relativity of 1916 provided the theoretical structure. The observations of Edwin Hubble in the 1920's provided the narrative. He saw that the universe was expanding, and thus if you worked backward logically that it must have had a start point – the infamous Big Bang as it is now known.

Few people understand physics at this level. It has been said that no-one except mathematicians and physicists understand anything beyond (roughly) page 27 of Stephen Hawking's bestseller "A Brief History of Time" because the concepts are so hard to grasp. Yet as Wertheim points out, Einstein remains one of the most popular icons of the 20th century (perhaps partly because he looks every inch the mad professor). At a visceral level, we seem to understand the importance of what he had to say. So although the reality of infinite space and time as a fourth dimension are hard to grasp, they have been accepted and inform our thinking and world view at a deep level.

Einstein challenged the Newtonian view of *absolute* space – a fixed and unchanging constant – and substituted for it *relative* space, where time and space varied according to the velocity of the observer. He gives us four dimensions, adding time to the other three. What is clear is that Einstein did not get to his theory in a cultural vacuum. Speculation about a fourth dimension had been prevalent since the 1860's. HG Wells used the idea in The Time Machine. Other scientists had already been pushing towards it. In 1908 Hermann Minkowski gave a famous lecture at the University of Cologne which began: "the views of space and time which I wish to lay before you have sprung from the soil of experimental physics, and therein lie their strength. They are radical. Henceforth space by itself, and time by itself, are doomed to fade away into mere shadows, and only a kind of union of the two will preserve an independent reality." Later he captured his thinking well by stating "nobody has ever noticed a place except at a time, or a time except at a place". Fellow physicist Hermann Weyl summarised the new thinking, "the scene of action of reality is…a four-dimensional world in which space and time are linked together indissolubly. However deep the chasm that separates the intuitive nature of space from time in our experience, nothing of this qualitative difference enters into the objective world which physics endeavours to crystallise out of direct experience. It is a four dimensional continuum, which is neither "space" or "time"."

Time as perspective

Artists too were now experimenting with dimensions to break free of traditions established in the fourteenth century. The key movement became known as cubism, and among its leading lights was Pablo Picasso (1881 – 1973). In 1907 he finished

Demoiselles d'Avignon, one of the most radical pictures of all time. Even now, almost a century later, it is not hard to imagine the shock that must have been caused to viewers of this painting of five women in a brothel. It was radical on several levels, introducing a new way of treating light and colour, an alternative to the classical norm for human bodies, and influences as eclectic as African art and El Greco. But the most radical and immediately striking thing about Les Demoiselles is its departure from previous ideas of representing space. In "Cubism"[10], art critic Edward Fry writes: "The treatment of space is, however, by far the most significant aspect of Les Demoiselles, especially in view of the predominant role of spatial problems in the subsequent development of cubism. The challenge facing Picasso was the creation of a new system of indicating three-dimensional relationships that would no longer be dependent on the convention of illusionistic, one point perspective." The solution lay with a method pioneered by Cezanne in which "he (Cezanne) organised his subjects according to the separate acts of perception he had experienced". For Picasso this took shape in portraying elements from different angles *as if they had been viewed over time*. Suddenly the route to portraying a fourth dimension lay open to those prepared to experiment, and art entered the 20th century.

So far we have focused on the relationship between figurative art and (the science of) space. It's interesting to see that in literature too a relationship can be tracked.

In Shakespeare's A Midsummer Night's Dream there is almost no mention of God, which is curious for a play written in such a religiously tense age. But there *is* a fairy domain alongside our world and tightly interwoven with it. In this case a space inhabited by spiritual beings is firmly tied to the known world. There is little of heaven here. Perhaps Shakespeare was already aware of the new currents of European thought. Just over a century later Jonathan Swift also envisaged imaginary people and lands in Gulliver's Travels, yet again very much tied to our physical environment but a little more distant: Gulliver goes on long voyages by boat to reach Lilliput, Brobdingnag and the land of the Houyhnhnms.

But in the 20th century some remarkable books – written for children – have shown us space alongside our "real" world – CS Lewis's Chronicles of Narnia are the first outstanding example[11]. Narnia is reached through a gateway which moves around. In one case it is a clothes cupboard in a big house, in another a door in a garden wall. Harry Potter and his chums get on board a train at Kings Cross on platform 9 3/4. Philip Pullman's Dark Materials trilogy also uses the idea of a cross-

---

[10] Oxford University Press, 1966

[11] It is true of course that fairy stories existed long before the 20th century, but I can think of none that show alternative worlds parallel to ours with different rules of time. Characters in fairy stories interact with our world directly, even if in a magical way.

ing place into other worlds – in this case one that can be opened by the wielder of special tool for cutting gateways in the air. Pullman extends the idea – there are numerous parallel worlds existing alongside each other – some similar, some very different from ours. Pullman and Lewis also, significantly, have time running to a different clock in their various worlds. "Narnian time flows differently from ours. If you spent a hundred years in Narnia, you would still come back to our world at the very same hour of the very same day on which you left. And then, if you went back to Narnia after spending a week here, you might find that a thousand Narnian years had passed, or only a day, or no time at all. You never know until you get there."[12]

What is this evidence of? That mankind yearns for a parallel world or worlds seems almost too obvious to point out, but most people are less aware that our concept of what those places might be and where they are has changed radically over history. And if contemporary representations in literature and art (in this case film) *are* significant, change is upon us again, now.

Digital Worlds

The best cultural evidence that our perceptions of space are once again shifting begins with the books of William Gibson. Gibson is an American novelist who writes (as defined by his publishers) science fiction. Science fiction has traditionally dealt with either space or some technological vision of the future on earth, usually both. Space in this context has usually meant *outer* space, that which is infinite and lies beyond our atmosphere. Men travel to other worlds which are distant and have distinct substance and reality.

Gibson brilliantly inverted this. His space also feels infinite but it is here on earth and contained within networks of computers across the planet. It is "Cyberspace" – Gibson is credited with inventing the term (and "Virtual Reality" too). The first book where he did this was Neuromancer[13]. It may not be the greatest work of literature from a technical point of view, but the depth of imagination more than makes up for any plot limitations. In it, Case, a "computer cowboy", makes his living by "jacking" himself into the network ("the Matrix" – yes Gibson invented that concept too). With his mind literally inside the network Case travels around it leaving his body (dismissively referred to as "meat") inanimate on the outside. Inside the Matrix, Case seeks out computers and storage facilities in order to penetrate them and steal data or alter code. The bigger and more important targets have defensive layers of "ICE" which Case has to peel away. What is remarkable about the descriptions are their architectural quality. When he first "jacks in" (plugs himself

---

[12] From "The Voyage of the Dawn Treader".
[13] Voyager

in directly) the data is revealed as a "fluid neon origami trick, the unfolding of his distanceless home, his country, transparent 3D chessboard extending to infinity. Inner eye opening to the stepped scarlet pyramid of the Eastern Seaboard Fission Authority burning beyond the green cubes of Mitsubishi Bank of America, and high and very far away he saw the spiral arms of military systems, forever beyond his reach." Cyberspace is colourful, infinite, and has a geographical reality. There are places, gates, pyramids, levels – in short *places*.

"Case punched for the Swiss banking sector, feeling a wave of exhilaration as cyberspace shivered, blurred, gelled. The Eastern Seaboard Fission Authority was gone, replaced by the cool geometric intricacy of Zurich commercial banking. He punched again, for Berne.

'Up,' the construct said. 'It'll be high'.

They ascended lattices of light, levels strobing, a blue flicker.

That'll be it, Case thought.

Wintermute was a simple cube of white light, that very simplicity suggesting extreme complexity.

'Don't look much, does it?' the Flatline said. 'But just you try and touch it'.

'I'm going in for a pass, Dixie.'

'Be my guest'.

Case punched to within four grid points of the cube. Its blank face, towering above him now, began to seethe with faint internal shadows, as though a thousand dancers whirled behind a vast sheet of frosted glass.

'Knows we're here' the Flatline observed.

Case punched again, once; they jumped forward by a single grid point.

A stippled gray circle formed on the face of the cube.

'Dixie…'

Mark Curtis

'Back off, fast.'

The gray area bulged smoothly, became a sphere, and detached itself from the cube.

Case felt the edge of the deck sting his palm as he slapped MAX REVERSE. The matrix lurched backward; they plunged down a twilit shaft of Swiss banks."

In 1984 this was revolutionary stuff, though the Matrix movies, inspired directly by Gibson's writings, make it seem less so now, as the idea of a vast invisible network all around us has passed into our collective consciousness. Remember that when Gibson wrote, the Internet barely existed and hackers were almost unknown. His Cyberspace becomes real through metaphor. As we navigate it with Case, this is the *only* way Gibson can help us visualise what he imagines. In fact at times the writing clearly breaks down as he struggles to break beyond what we know. You can feel the author straining to describe the utterly new. It is very similar to the points at which Giotto, centuries before, distorts his new found mastery of perspective in order to accommodate his medieval vision of celestial space.

Infinity has been a disaster for heaven[14]. If physical space fills everything available, for ever, there is no room for anything beyond. Because there is no beyond. With no spiritual space in the western scientific tradition by which we are now dominated, there is literally no space for the spirit. Some people have speculated that cyberspace could play this role, and that this partly explains its popularity. "People will only adopt a technology if it resonates with a perceived need. For a technology to be successful, a latent desire must be there to be satisfied. The sheer scale of interest in cyberspace suggests that there is not only an intense desire at work here, but also a profound psychosocial vacuum that many people are hoping the Internet might fill."[15] These visions are often twinned with ideas that sooner or later we will be able to replicate not only our DNA but also our thought patterns in software – a "construct" in Gibson's language. This of course would enable us to live forever in the matrix, unconcerned by the decay of our bodies which we would have escaped forever.

Of course true virtual reality has barely entered the lives of most people yet. In the early 1990's it looked much closer. At the time I wrote a script for two virtual reality experiences using machines from a British company called Virtuality to bring

---

[14] Of course I'm not including parts of the world where religious orthodoxy denies the validity the science it does not care for: I'm told this even includes a substantial part of the US population which embraces creationism.

[15] Wertheim

---

it to "life". A heavy headset linked to platforms where users were either seated or standing (in the latter case they could also pick things up with a glove). The most compelling part of the experiences involved dramatic shifts of scale. We gave users a mouse eye view of the world. Wrapped in their goggles it was amusing and weird to see them duck when a giant pixelated boot descended from the sky in their virtual world. Although most people have never experienced this or anything like it, nowadays they can imagine it.

You cannot travel into a fresco because it remains a point in time and space, even if it does tell a story spread over the whole chapel. You can follow a film through a limited amount of time, say two hours – but in most circumstances only in one direction. Virtual reality however gives you – potentially – infinite space you can explore in your time. The idea of this has passed irretrievably into public consciousness. Once again, this changes the way we relate to each other and the world, and will have largely unpredictable consequences.

We can however already see one spatial change that digital media has brought to us: and that is the degree to which we are now implicitly and explicitly connected *to each other*. Mobile phones do this more than anything else, because now our connectedness travels with us everywhere we go. This is the profound force that is re-shaping us. The network of our connections is becoming woven into our physical lives. We had thought that a new digital landscape all of its own was springing into existence, one which existed in "hyperspace", which had its own map. This was William Gibson's vision. To some extent via the Internet it is true. But now we have to factor in mobile too, and it looks like mobile is actually mapping the virtual on to the real world.

PART ONE
The Social Price Of New Technology

Chapter Three
Going Mobile

On its own, the Internet would have been a major new technology. The arrival of mobile phones at more or less the same time has guaranteed a period of huge social change. In this chapter and the next, we start to look at why going mobile makes us part of the network, permanently linked in. We also explore how new layers of information will arrive, attached both to the places and things around us, and see in what ways all this is changing our behaviour.

Always on

Wireless has untethered the digital revolution and utterly changed its landscape. The speed with which mobile phones have penetrated day to day lives across the world (more so in Europe and Asia than in the US) is astonishing and scarcely require statistics for proof – you can hear it in the warble of ringtones across private and public space, see it in the hand to ear posture of a thousand passers-by each day.

Craig Kanarick, one of the founders of Razorfish, used to say that mankind was originally nomadic, had then discovered the plough, the hearth and settled down. Now mobile was untethering the human race again, allowing us to pursue our lifestyles with less reference to geographical anchors. It is a characteristically sweeping view of history, and open to the criticism that it may be true for a busy international executive, but not for "normal people". But the evidence is that, although not everyone may regard themselves as unfettered road warriors, mobile is changing habits for many.

Any European parent with teenage children who own mobiles has discovered this in the last three to five years. 70% of 15 – 19 year olds in Britain agree "I like to be contactable on my mobile all the time" compared with 37% of average adults[16]. The mobile device has caused a re-negotiation of parent/child relationships. With

---

[16] The Henley Centre

---

two teenage daughters, I write as one who knows.

The phone has become a focal point of their lives. The changes are many, main-ly subtle, yet combining to a greater whole.

The mobile phone has become the organising tool of life for teenagers[17]. It con-nects them 24 hours a day with their network of friends, and thankfully, their parents too. All this, no matter where they are. It would have been unthinkable 20 years ago:

- that parents could talk to children at school, directly
- that romances could be carried on by SMS during school hours, in lessons
- that parents could phone children to find out where they are at the weekend
- that teenagers could text each other (it's silent) at 2 in the morning

and so on. These changes seem small – but they affect the surface pattern of daily life. Looming underneath is a substantial reorientation.

A new catchphrase appeared in the wireless world a few years ago – "always on". The concept referred to the promise that GPRS technology would deliver hand-sets that were always connected to the Internet, bringing with them the benefit of speedier mobile access to goldmines of information. As it happens, connection times are still pretty slow and "always on" has yet to deliver its explicit promise where the handsets are concerned.

The truth now is that the devices which are always on are *us*, and we nearly always have devices on us. We were getting there bit by byte with the Internet, but the ubiquity of mobile has locked the switch in place.

We expect almost everyone to have mobiles (not unreasonably – over 80% of the UK adult population do). We expect them to be on most of the time – or at the least to be checked frequently enough to generate a return call rapidly. Our most important contacts are stored in an address book – on the phone. Mobile phones tap into something very deep in our psyche: according to Unisys the banking and credit card industries claim that it takes an average of 26 hours for a user to (notice and) report a lost wallet. But the average time taken to report a lost mobile phone is 68 minutes[18]. Surely, rationally, the loss of the wallet is potentially more serious? No wonder many think the two will merge shortly.

For the next generation this is life. I'd guess – through experience – that taking a teenagers' phone away from them is now the biggest sanction 21st century parents can invoke against bad behaviour. When phones are stolen, it is interesting to ob-serve that what most people miss is not the hardware itself (usually insured anyway)

---

[17] It's not just teenagers: Mattel plan to introduce a Barbie phone in 2005 for girls aged 8 – 14 (parents can control it through a web site)

[18] Unisys M-Commerce presentation at IBC's M-Commerce London 15-16.4,2003

Mark Curtis

but their contact list (it's a hassle to rebuild) and their stored text messages (usually for sentimental reasons).

The sense of always on is redoubled by other new media beyond mobile: Internet based messenger services also feature address books (buddy lists) and are most popular with children and teenagers (and are now making inroads into corporations too). The mainstream media have absorbed the lessons fast: radio and TV channels use SMS as a primary method of feedback. Big Brother discovered that many viewers watch TV with their phones within easy reach, hence voting by voice or text was a natural development.

The consequence is that people are increasingly aware that they are virtually present in address books, e-mail servers and even on CCTV screens and videotapes (the average urban UK individual is recorded 30 times a day by CCTV cameras). We are extending ourselves into Cyberspace, beyond the constraints of our bodies, or as William Gibson would have it, our meat based selves. This cuts both ways: I am both constantly available to the network, and others likewise. Using e-mail I can project myself thousands of miles away with a few key strokes. I can contribute to a discussion forum whose actual location I have no idea of, and inflict my views on potentially millions of other people.

We are becoming distributed beings. Without our new conceptions of space this could not happen. Mobile makes the trend explicit.

The role that wireless communication would play in the future was largely missed by Gibson in Neuromancer – at one point Case uses public telephones at an airport, which today feels as much of an anachronism as if he was caught smoking a pipe. In 1984 it passed unnoticed. Margaret Wertheim in the Pearly Gates of Cyberspace, written in 1998, also takes no account of wireless in her history of space.

The significance of wireless is that the network, cyberspace, the matrix – call it what you will – is now all around us in our environment – mapped to real geographic places[19]. Led by Gibson and the early Internet gurus with their muds and moos (acronyms for digital communities of the time), we had thought that it would be an infinite kind of inner space and much of that vision of the Internet still stands. Now however we are discovering that cyberspace might be more closely linked to the everyday physical world.

This is mobile: as a communications technology it has slipped alongside our everyday lives very easily, reflecting, reporting, amplifying our daily actions. Researcher Sadie Plant comments: "All around the world, the mobile has become

---

[19] UK SMS-to-Screen provider Impulse has installed SMS chat screens into nightclubs and discos all over the UK. In February 2004 they had over 100,000 SMS text messages sent to the screens – source Tomi Ahonen

associated with a handful of phrases which recur like samples in a global dance track. These include "on my way", "on the bus", "on the train', and other answers to a question which is now so common that it has come to define the mobile age: 'where are you?' If this is the perfect mobile question, the perfect answer is 'on the mobile'.[20]

In fact, the device (and the network) already knows where you are.

Become the map

Someone once said that in the act of walking, you become part of the map. With a mobile phone, that is becoming literally true.

By measuring the time it takes for a signal to reach your phone and come back, a network operator such as Orange can approximate how far you are from a transmission mast. If they triangulate your position from three masts, they can get a surprisingly good fix in urban areas – perhaps down to 200 metres or so. In areas with a lower density of masts, like the Outer Hebrides, the accuracy may be no better than 35 miles.

However with global positioning chips (GPS) accuracy can be considerably improved down to 5 metres or less. GPS chips are already in many devices: mountaineers and walkers are familiar with them through specialist navigation handsets. The US government has mandated that all mobile phones sold in the US must facilitate with location details the answering of emergency service calls – for instance to locate victims of accidents or crime. The accuracy that is demanded makes it likely that GPS will increasingly become standard on phones at least in the US. It'll come in Europe and Asia too.

Location based services are considered by many people in the mobile industry to be the next big thing. The thinking is simple: if we know where people are via their phone, how can we enhance the services we offer them?

Initially a lot of nonsense has been talked about how this would enable retailers to spot you as you walk past and beam marketing messages into your mobile to entice you into the store – "Hey! Fancy a Big Mac? You're only 20 metres from one right now". This vision takes no account of consumer preferences and is unlikely to be taken seriously by any marketer with their brain switched on (if we are wrong on this one the consequences hardly bear thinking about).[21]

More thoughtful services have emerged. Orange and other operators offer the ability via WAP to find your nearest restaurant, cashpoint, cinema, pub and many other locations too. It's reasonably accurate, but not perfect – even in central London

---

[20] From "On the Mobile", a booklet written for Motorola
[21] The 1994 novel "Snow Crash" by Neal Stephenson does imagine it.

a miss is literally as good as a mile. But the ability to refine your location helps narrow choices down, and these services will improve. Zingo is a taxi service that allows you to hail a black cab in London by mobile. Their "GPS and phone location technology identifies where you are and connects you directly to the nearest available Zingo taxi driver". Anyone who has frozen trying to get a cab in London after ten at night in December will realise what a good idea this is.

With a bit of imagination, it's not hard to see other services emerge over the next few years which use location as a springboard. The idea I am about to describe was developed with colleagues as part of our work, but similar ideas are being both talked about and developed across the world. We called it "Digital Graffiti".

Digital Graffiti brings the physical and virtual worlds closer together by giving mobile users the opportunity to "tag" locations with "messages". To bring it to life, we imagined a fictional user some time not very far into the future…

rich calls it "tagging the city"…and since it's his city why not? On Friday night he walks right across downtown from work to the first bar of the night and sees hotspots that no-one can with just their eyes – like a sort of a 4th dimension is how he describes it to his girlfriend.

Tonight he sets the filter to alert him to tags laid in the last hour – its busier each week and market square is almost too hot. He can see JAZ45's trail almost as clearly as if he was tracking footprints – this guy's good – funny, edgy, avoids the usual iwozhere smiley clichés. So when he says check out the girl with the leopard skin pill box hat in Starbucks rich doesn't hesitate. Hmm…Giggling, rich adds a tag endorsing JEZ's taste. He knows that 2 messages so close will begin to attract a lot more soon. But he doesn't stay in Starbucks – he's read too many tags about their 3rd world coffee purchasing and he knows that Starbucks HATES tagging. Tough.

First to the bar, his friends are late. So rich leaves a tag ("I was here where were you? Your round I think!") – and strolls down to the waterfront to watch the boats go by while he waits for the others to turn up. And there it is again – the most beautiful poetry on his screen – as if someone is writing it down here everyday (they are). It lightens up his mood and he saves it to show his girlfriend later. Or maybe he sends it to her now along with a photo of the river.

Why would anyone want digital graffiti?

* It allows a new kind of self expression
* It's a new way for social networks to talk
* It has subversive overtones: users can see things not everyone can, and have the ability to tag institutions
* Creative content will be a form of street entertainment

- Messages might be useful
- It's not visually polluting
- It 's a new art form
- It adds a new layer to our physical lives

An idea like this might not be that far away using existing technology. Graffiti could be text, audio (music clips, voice messages, ambient sounds), photographs, graphics, animations, video. A web site could be provided for creation of content, from where files could be uploaded to the mobile handset (via MMS) or accessed directly (via WAP).

Possibly a motion sensor in the device, combined with a choice of colour, could allow users to "spray" a design in the air, view it on their screen and save it/tag a location with it.

Graffiti could be a combination of all of the above – and might include, for instance, a comment on the place, a photograph of myself, a clip from some music plus a graphical signature. Users will be able to leave graffiti anywhere it is supported by a mobile network. They might do so to say: "I've been here" or "these are my feelings about this place".

Variables could include size of graffiti and lifetime. Users might pay more for a BIG graffiti, which would be delivered to more users or prioritised in display. Users might pay more for a graffiti which lasts longer.

The functionality to update graffiti remotely could be included: for instance using the web I could add a photo later to illustrate a point I wished to make (e.g." this is what a decent pizza looks like – avoid this joint"). Each tag could have its own unique ID created by the system which permitted this. At the extreme, users could be permitted to create and tag remotely using, for example, postcodes or a map.

Users could be alerted to tags with a screensaver/in idle mode (perhaps given a taste of the content) or via standard message alerts (sms, wap push, mms)

Assuming that current cell sizes may be the minimum accuracy, and that the system achieves high usage – some locations will become cluttered with tags and therefore some sort of filtering will be required. We believe the vast majority of users will filter to their interests. This could be by:

- Popularity (which tags/authors are most looked at?)
- Time (which tags are the most recent)
- Paid for (which tags have been purchased as BIG)
- Subject matter
- Media used (only show me tags with pictures)
- Author (show me tags by my friends/authors I like)
- Random carousel (effectively no filter)

Mark Curtis

Digital graffiti will almost certainly demonstrate some very interesting emergent properties[22]. For sure some people will abuse it and leave offensive tags. We expect the system therefore to have peer review: for instance a three strikes and you're out could automatically delete tags if three people object to a tag. Serious objections could be registered and traced to eliminate illegal activity.

In essence the concept is about the private reading of public spaces. So why not extend it by making public display part of the idea? Large screens could be linked to the tagging system showing material on a carousel. A more interesting route could be T-shirts which react to tags in the location.

We can't say for sure that digital graffiti will ever form part of the urban landscape – though we think that something like it will. What it shows is the way in which virtual or cyberspace will increasingly be mapped to the real world, rather than existing in a distant and intangible firmament of its own.

Thinking things?

Location based services are dependent on people carrying phones. But what if things – rather than people – also had a digital identity that they could carry with them? That technology too is also with us already. Its best known manifestation is RFID – radio frequency identification. RFID tags or chips, some no bigger than a grain of rice, allow remote tracking of anything that they are attached to. It's a big step forward: previous tracking devices required line of sight to operate. But because RFID uses radio, a scanner or transmitter can read information off a tag up to 90 feet away. In other words they allow dumb things like a case of beer to identify themselves. The technology has been around for some time – many people have heard of it – but only now are prices for the chips reaching a low enough level to allow mass usage. Prices quoted vary from 40 US cents to $1 per chip.

The commercial use that is creating the most excitement is on the supply side: retailers and manufacturers are exploring how they can use RFID to stop theft, introduce tighter stock control and respond more rapidly to sales trends. If your products tell you when they leave the store in real time, you know when and where to send new supplies. WALMART, the aggressive US retailer, had mandated that by the middle of this decade, their Top 100 suppliers should have RFID tags on all cases and pallets delivered.

There is gathering media attention around RFID as consumer campaigners have made the connection that if companies can track things, they can also track their consumers. This is causing a storm – especially in the US. Consumer protection

---

[22] Stephen Johnson's book "Emergence" (Penguin) explains brilliantly how systems develop their characteristic properties.

groups led by CASPIAN (Consumers Against Supermarket Privacy Invasion and Numbering) are fearful that RFID tags could be put to sinister uses by unscrupulous companies. They claim to have forced Gillette to back off a trial of RFID in razor-blade packaging.

According to Newsweek, Katherine Albrecht, "a Harvard doctoral student who has been leading the charge…owns a bookshelf full of material about oppressive 20th-century governments that exploited available technologies".[23]

It's hard to see why RFID is such a threat, in this context. Why should I care if Gillette knows how many blades I've bought? How exactly are they going to scan my bathroom? What happens when I throw the packaging in the bin…will they track it into the rubbish cart and so on to the landfill site? Caspian are very unclear on precisely what the threat is. Anyway, it seems probable that supermarkets will "kill" the chip as it leaves to provide safeguards, and industry experts estimate that it could be ten years until the tags arrive on the products we actually buy.

Nonetheless, technologies like location awareness and RFID are weaving cyberspace yet more closely into our lives, bringing us alongside a parallel space of information.

Unless you are fascinated by supply logistics, or a privacy nut, it may be more interesting to consider what happens in a world where technology makes physical things all around us interactive. In other words, when the physical and digital world become enmeshed with each other and you can manipulate information through real objects rather than a two dimensional screen on your PC, TV or phone.

The Massachusetts Institute of Technology (MIT) calls this Tangible Bits and has a whole research group dedicated to exploring possibilities. As the head of the group says "pixels impoverish the senses".[24]

LoveMe Dolls

If you could use more senses than seeing and hearing to communicate and interact, what might this be like? One playful solution is LoveMe Dolls.[25]

A LoveMe doll is a small physical representation of a person that's important to you. The doll might represent a child, a parent, a boyfriend, a lover, or a colleague. The doll is not only a reminder of a person; it's a dedicated communication channel that allows easy exchange of meaningful information. We imagine the dolls would be sold in pairs to represent a relationship. They are cheap, very easy to operate and they can be personalised quickly.

---

[23] Newsweek 29th September 2003
[24] The Feature.com October 2003
[25] Again, this is work developed with my colleagues at Fjord.

Mark Curtis

LoveMe dolls are all the things that mobile phones are not: they are personal reminders of people, symbols of relationships, they are soft, durable, and their behaviour is slightly unpredictable.

Tim and Susie have been married for five years. They have a 7-year-old son, Johnny. It was Johnny's birthday two weeks ago, and Susie bought a pair of LoveMe dolls for Johnny and herself. The initial reason to buy Johnny a doll was to remind Johnny of his mum when he's at school, because Johnny is still not completely comfortable with being away from home all day, and the physical representation of his mum would provide a real sense of comfort and security.

Two weeks later Johnny and Susie are actually exchanging several messages a day via their dolls. Susie usually initiates the messages with the standard "Thinking of you!" alert, and Johnny answers simply by squeezing the doll once, sending a generic "Yes (I hear you)" message back. Susie has also started to use the doll for more practical purposes, like asking Johnny "Will you need your football kit tomorrow?" Johnny simply replies with one squeeze (yes!) or two squeezes (no!).

What Susie doesn't yet know is that Johnny has used part of his weekly allowance to buy a new long fur skin (Neanderthal-style) for the Susie-doll. He is also making Susie do funny noises and strange moves in school, all to the amusement and adoration of his friends.

Susie's doll of Johnny has a photo of him displayed on the screen, and Tim is watching it with amusement as this representation of his son occasionally lights up and bleeps, then displays the message "Love you, mum". After a few weeks Tim is starting to get a bit jealous of all this bonding between his wife and his son. He feels a bit sidelined.

One day Tim comes home with an advanced LoveMe doll pair, and gives one of them to Susie as a surprise present. The doll is cuddly and soft, and it has a pin stuck to it: "the world's best husband". When she turns on the doll, it whispers "Hellooooo babyyyy..." in a suggestive manner. It makes her giggle. The colour screen is displaying a slideshow with 10 photos of Tim and special moments that they've shared. She also discovers that Tim has programmed the doll with some pre-defined messages, allowing Susie and Tim to exchange personal messages simply by squeezing or holding the dolls tight. How sweet of him!

Soon Tim has a new habit: He's holding and squeezing the Susie-doll when he is in meetings at work. The warmth of his hand triggers messages sent to Susie. When Susie replies with loving messages, Tim sneaks the Susie-doll into his pocket. The increased warmth triggers more intensive messages!

One thing that Tim didn't expect, however, was Susie's use of the doll when she's annoyed with him. One day when Tim had again forgotten to pay their broadband bill, leaving her without a computer connection at home, Susie throws her Tim-doll into the wall, releasing some aggression. At work Tim's Susie-doll suddenly jumps

20 cm into the air. Wow, something's really going on with Susie he thinks, and gives her a call. Later in the evening they meet for dinner at a restaurant, and they put the dolls next to each other. The dolls make cute sounds, and the naughty suggestions that the dolls seem to make to each other make them laugh, and it's easier to put the issue from earlier behind them.

After a while Tim discovers the location feature of the dolls, and starts to trace the movement of his son and wife when he's at work. Today he's checking Susie's location on the web before he leaves work. He sees that she's on the way back from the gym, and gives her a call to ask her to pick up some coriander from the green grocers for the Indian dinner he's going to cook.

Why would anyone want a LoveMe doll?

- The doll is a physical manifestation of an important relationship, a reminder of someone; it's a meaningful and functional extension of the personal photo you keep in your wallet
- It's an alternative to jewellery and other signs of commitment between people in relationships
- It's a "direct line" to and from the person it represents
- It's not as disruptive as a phone
- It's small, light, and durable enough to be carried with you anywhere you go
- It's cheaper to buy and use than a mobile phone, making it a perfect object for young children
- Playing with and using the doll is fun and addictive

So how do you interact with the doll?

It only has one button for operating it. It's a joystick or a navi-key that allows you to navigate between elements, and make selections. There might be a handful of pre-defined messages (I love you/Thinking of you/See you soon/Call me) that you can select between. There are no keys on the doll. Instead you can trigger behaviour and send messages by squeezing the doll or by warming it in your hand. The doll will also sense certain movement. If it's thrown against a wall sound feedback and an outgoing message can be triggered. The doll is also aware of the physical proximity of its pair: if two friends meet and they put their dolls together the dolls might make happy sounds and bounce around for a bit.

The dolls and their behaviour can be programmed and controlled from mobile phones. The buyer of dolls would be able to easily assign attributes to the dolls. Attributes might be things like doll name, sex, age, type of relationship (father/ sister/lover). The type of relationship would affect the behaviour of a doll. For ex-

Mark Curtis

ample, when two friends put their dolls together, the dolls might bounce and make happy/silly comments, but when a woman puts her doll next to her new boyfriend's, the dolls might start flirting! From your mobile phone you can also easily change the default messages of the dolls. The SMS allowance of a doll can also be controlled from a mobile phone.

The interaction with a doll will not necessarily have to be precise and goal-orientated. Human interaction is not always precise, and signs can be interpreted many different ways. Lots of interaction and communication is used to maintain and enhance relationships. The same is the case with the dolls. Stroking/heating/squeezing can all trigger feedback and messages, but exactly when and how this works can be left a bit fuzzy. The interaction design, the physical qualities of the dolls, the graphics and the sounds will all communicate soft, responsive and ultimately human qualities. The behaviour of the doll includes serendipity. The dolls can surprise and engage you in new ways, in ways unimaginable for computers and mobile phones.

Sometimes you might want to make more significant enhancements to the dolls. Simple media like photos, slide shows or messages displayed randomly can be created on a computer and delivered to the doll via MMS. The media packs will automatically install on the doll, and they require no physical interaction with the doll. The update of and addition to the dolls can happen remotely, creating nice surprises for the keeper of the doll.

The physical alteration or dress-up of the doll is a key element. You can buy different skins that represent the nature of the relationship, and you might choose to dress and undress a doll depending on your situation and location. Your doll could wear:

- a glittering party dress for an evening outing
- a casual denim skin for daytime use
- a kinky black latex skin for your despised mother in law
- a simple velcro skin that allows you to stick on many meters of additional textile

Also, since the dolls have soft skins you can easily pin buttons to them, or attach stickers. Weird? Yes, but much of what we do in the 21st century would look bizarre to our great grandfathers.

There might be a range of different dolls to choose from. You can buy a simple, cheap doll for your 7-year old kid, and if it's lost you can quickly replace it. Or you can choose a top-end doll for your new partner – it's a clear sign of commitment (best not to lose it then).

Fantasy? Maybe. But I believe that LoveMe Dolls and Digital Graffiti both illustrate a near future where our changing perceptions of space create new digital communications possibilities – and vice versa. Some of these will be useful, fun and life enhancing. Judge for yourself whether the two examples are any or all of these. Others will be no better than a distraction. And distraction is now the issue to turn to.

PART ONE
The Social Price Of New Technology

Chapter Four
Distraction Technologies

In the last chapter we saw how we are becoming "always on", and so are the things and places around us. We are now going to start to look at how this extraordinary potential for communication is creating new social behaviour patterns in front of our eyes, distracted as we are by the potential for personal attention from somewhere else. Will video calls demand further adaptation? In extreme cases, we can become addicted to distraction. Perhaps we see this reflected in the media. Should we legislate to create the right kind of response to these new challenges? Or should we instead debate our new social behaviours and rethink them, finding new strategies to deal with technology that is not going away any time soon?

Here we are – in a world where digital has created a parallel sense of space where we, and everything else, are always on. It's very distracting. TV, the Internet and now mobile phones bring the digital world into our own space and fill it. Emptiness is hard to achieve.[26]

Marshall McLuhan understood the potential of the phone in "Understanding Media".[27]

"In the 1920's a popular song was "All Alone by the Telephone, All Alone Feeling Blue". Why should the phone create an intense feeling of loneliness? Why should we feel compelled to answer a ringing public phone when we know the call cannot concern us? Why does a phone ringing on the stage create instant tension? Why is that tension so very much less for an unanswered phone in a movie scene? The answer to all of these questions is that the phone is a participant form that demands a partner…it simply will not act as a background instrument like a radio."

The phone is very insistent – we cannot leave it alone. This is partly explained by McLuhan's theory that the phone demands a partner and partly because we all wish to feel wanted. In fact it is entertaining, involving and two way. Calls, text mes-

---

[26] And perhaps is becoming the new luxury, e.g.: the rise of spas, flotation tanks, meditation etc…
[27] MIT Press

sages and e-mail satisfy that need.

Until recently, so did the trad[28]itional letter post. WH Auden captured it perfectly in his poem Night Mail which celebrated the Post Office mail train service which has just last year been phased out (too inefficient apparently). It begins…

"This is the Night Mail crossing the border,
Bringing the cheque and the postal order,
Letters for the rich, letters for the poor,
The shop at the corner and the girl next door."

And ends insightfully

"And none will hear the postman's knock
Without a quickening of the heart,
For who can bear to feel himself forgotten?"

(W H Auden)

It's hard to imagine a similar eulogy to e-mail or SMS. However they are more distracting than the post, which only arrived twice a day at known times.

The distraction of a mobile is caused not just by it ringing, but also by its *potential* to ring. When a mobile is slapped down on a table between two people in a café, that potential is made implicit in a way that cannot help but impact on their (immediate) relationship.

If M Scott Peck is right, this is very damaging. He writes persuasively in "The Road Less Travelled"[29] a 1978 classic of the self-help genre, that "discipline is the basic set of tools we require to solve life's problems…what are these tools…that I call discipline? There are four: delaying of gratification, acceptance of responsibility, dedication to truth, and balancing."

The problem is that digital media strike at the heart of the first of these. If I elevate the opportunity to feed my need to answer the phone, or read my e-mail while I am in a meeting, above focusing on the person and matter at hand, then I am avoiding the immediate issue in preference for the *gratification* of getting that call, reading this text. All kinds of social problems can come from this if I fail to engage properly or deeply with those (physically) close to me. That essential and still underrated skill – listening -goes out of the window, riding on the belief that the world

---

[28] Which also meant that its arrival could slot into the plan of your day. This isn't possible with e-mail, unless you discipline yourself only to look at it at set times. When the post has come, that's it.
[29] Arrow

Mark Curtis

a fingertap or two away may just be more interesting than my current reality.

Writer and researcher Dr Sadie Plant puts it well: "The receipt of a public call tends to be met by one of three responses. These are **flight**, in which users immediately move to absent themselves from their social situation: **suspension**, in which recipients stay put, but stop whatever they are doing for the duration of a call and effectively cut themselves off from their environment: and **persistence**, in which users stay put and engaged with the actual world, as far as possible carrying on with whatever they were doing before they made or took the call. All these responses run some risk that people who are present at the time will feel abandoned by the person who has answered the mobile, and in so doing has opted to be answerable to the device rather than to them".[30] There can hardly be anyone in the UK who would not perceive the truth in this simple analysis. It's scarcely surprising stuff and yet although we know it, many of us seem unable to moderate our behaviour accordingly. This is testimony to the power of a connected hand held device to disrupt our relationships. And of course, we've just become habituated to it, in an astonishingly short time. A colleague, Celia, comments that if she sat down with someone and they turned their phone off, she would now feel it was a sign they were going to give her full, undivided attention. It is questionable if this is the norm any more in many settings.

This is not to say that objections do not occur, that groups do not form their own tacit rules for mobile use that meet the needs of members. Inhibitions do definitely exist. I am not trying to paint a picture of a universal lack of mobile restraint. The insistence of the mobile is resented and some simple restrictions have emerged – for instance the banning of mobile use in restaurants, train carriages and pubs. One old half timbered pub I know well, the Fleur de Lys in Pilley, Hampshire has the burnt out shell of a Motorola handset nailed to the wall in a sort of mediaeval warning to carriers of a 21st century plague.

Being There

Certainly people in pubs shouting into their phone can be annoying. One is always suspicious that a degree of ostentatious performance is underway. Technology can play a display role. This was captured wonderfully in the programme Trigger Happy TV where Dom Joly is seen on trains, in bars and walking down the street with a truly giant phone clamped to his ear, yelling banalities into it. The point is not only that he is rude – which he magnificently is by virtue of intruding on others in a public space, but that he is enjoying the message that it sends. Look at me, I'm important – places to go! People to see!

Sadie Plant again – her research team observed people at bars in central London and found that 60% of lone women had a mobile on show. In this case the need

---

[30] in "On The Mobile" – a booklet written for Motorola

fulfilled appears to be very different to Joly's caricature – "many women saw this reflecting their own experience of the mobile as a valuable means of keeping unwanted attentions at bay. A mobile even projects an image of self containment, and can even legitimise solitude: I'm not alone, I'm with my mobile phone." It also perhaps signals that she is about to be met – either in person or by someone coming to her via a phone call.

The confusion of private and public space is at the heart of this issue. It can be very hard to deal with a call that places conversational demands on the recipient, which are strongly at odds with their context. This works both ways: the call can intrude on the environment or the context can affect the call. For instance it's hard to have an emotionally charged conversation, or negotiate a contract, on a crowded train. You don't want people to overhear, yet the caller may not be empathetic to the problem. Vice versa, taking a business call at home and then trying to muffle your dog barking or baby wailing can be a trial of nerves. Why do it at all? Because of the insistence of the device and the fact that we feel the need to be always on.

The trend is already being observed and commented on. Paul Goldberger, a NY Times art and architecture critic, wrote

"When you are in Paris you expect to wallow in its Parisness, to feel that everyone walking up the Boulevard Montparnasse is as totally and completely there as the lampposts, the kiosks, the facade of the Brasserie Lipp – and that they could be no place else. So we want it to be in every city, in every kind of place. When you are in a forest, you want to experience its woodsiness; when you are on the beach, you want to feel connected to sand and surf.

This is getting harder to do, not because these special places don't exist or because urban places have come to look increasingly alike... you no longer feel that being in one place cuts you off from other places. Technology has been doing this for a long time, of course – remember when people communicated with Europe by letter and it took a couple of weeks to get a reply? Now we're upset if we have to send a fax because it takes so much longer than e-mail.

But the cell phone has changed our sense of place more than faxes and computers and e-mail because of its ability to intrude into every moment in every possible place. When you walk along the street and talk on a cell phone, you are not on the street sharing the communal experience of urban life. You are in some other place – someplace at the other end of your phone conversation. You are there, but you are not there... Now that is increasingly true of almost every person on almost every street in almost every city. You are either on the phone or carrying one, and the moment it rings you will be transported out of real space into a virtual realm...[31]

---

[31] Goldberger slightly overstates this to make his point. In truth it's not one or the other (real or virtual) but both

Mark Curtis

The great offense of the cell phone in public is not the intrusion of its ring, although that can be infuriating when it interrupts a tranquil moment. It is the fact that even when the phone does not ring at all, and is being used quietly and discreetly, it renders a public place less public. It turns the boulevardier into a sequestered individual, the flaneur into a figure of privacy. And suddenly the meaning of the street as a public place has been hugely diminished."[32]

Interestingly text does not confuse private and public domains so much, which is one explanation of its popularity with teenagers, who often feel a greater need to be discrete than most adults – for whatever reason. The arrival tone is a disruptive signal to be sure, but text conversations are certainly less obvious, even though they can be just as subtly disruptive. At least text doesn't shout. Plant believes that the private/public space mix is also the cause of difficulties people have with the level they speak at while on a mobile: an explanation for Dom Joly's dysfunction.

For observation of body language in this field I'm going to turn once again to Sadie Plant and quote extensively – she says it better than I can and I like her terminology.

"In response to the novel physical and psychological demands made by mobiles, people have introduced new stances, gestures and bodily movements to their everyday behaviour, changing the ways in which the body, the fingers, the thumbs, then hands and the eyes are used while making and taking mobile calls or sending and receiving mobile messages. Many of these actions and positions have become familiar to observers all over the world, and it is possible to articulate some of the more marked and conspicuous elements of this new body language.

Public makers and takers of calls tend to assume one of two bodily postures, both of which extend and reflect the broader observations about introverted and extroverted use. Those who adopt the **speakeasy** pose keep their heads thrown back and their necks upright, giving out an air of self-assurance and single-minded refusal to be distracted by the outside world. This is an open and expansive position, confident and unapologetic.

The spacemaker is rather more introverted and closed, a gesture of withdrawal, particularly in the context of a busy city street. It provides ways of carving out a private arena, establishing a closed circuit from which all external interference is deliberately and visibly excluded. The head is bowed and inclined towards the phone, and the whole body may be slightly leaning, as though into the phone or towards the disembodied voice. The spacemaker may walk around in circles, stopping and starting in a bodily response to the conversation on the mobile. Many mobile users in this spacemaking mode seek out and improvise such places of comfort and relaxation from which to take or make their calls. It was observed in the course of this

---

[32] Metropolis Magazine, November 2003

research that many people sitting down in public spaces – at café tables, for example, or on park benches – tend to draw their bodies up, take their feet off the ground, or otherwise create a feeling of safety and withdrawal. Alternatively the body may be turned away from the world, perhaps towards a corner, or even – as observed on several occasions in Hong Kong, an unused telephone kiosk – as though to protect the conversation...

There are also variations in the ways in which people's eyes respond to a mobile call. Some mobile users adopt **the scan**, in which the eyes tend to be lively, darting around, perhaps making fleeting contact with people in the vicinity, as though they were searching for the absent face of the person to whom the call is made. With **the gaze**, the eyes tend to focus on a single point, or else to gaze into the distance, as though in an effort to conjure the presence of the disembodied voice."

Plant and her research team have captured well some of the new social behaviours associated with mobile devices. I would add the observation that people (especially teenagers) fiddle with their phones incessantly and often without seeming purpose, turning them over repeatedly in the palm of their hand. Maybe it fulfills the same nervous fidget role that cigarettes do for smokers.[33]

What most of these actions have in common is the shift in the perception of space: in public we can be transported by a ringtone to a different place. The effort to accommodate this shift is apparent in the contortions of the pacemaker, the distant focus of the gaze. Some may contend that this is not new. Staring into middle distance while being on a phone is hardly unheard of on the traditional, fixed line kind of phone. The body language of withdrawal would have been familiar 1000 years ago to anyone who received letters and wished to contemplate the contents in private.

The crucial difference now is of course that mobiles are with us wherever we go, and form a key pillar of the "always on" life. So habits and actions that were previously confined to the home and perhaps the workplace, are now instinctive companions on top of a hill on a walk with the family, in the train with strangers, in the pub with your mates after the football match.

What we do with our physical selves reveals our mental map: we are now connected to distant people and places continuously. When those connections become active our effort to manage disembodied travel becomes a physical one. Those around us see and understand. We are somewhere else, and yet not.

Mobile phones have been a particular success in Japan – not just for calls but also messaging, taking and sending pictures, and mobile use of the Internet. There are lots of theories as to why – among them that Japanese society is more restrictive and less comfortable with face to face. It is thought that mobile messaging allows

---

[33] Could it be mildly addictive?

Mark Curtis

Japanese teenagers in particular to be more comfortable with, for instance, flirting and to evade parental monitoring (harder to do on a fixed landline with one phone in the home.)

Two researchers – Mizuko Ito and Daisuke Okabe are doing interesting work exploring this new terrain. They contend that although mobile is breaking down social norms it is also building new ones.[34] They describe the "augmented flesh meet", where phones are used to define at a late stage where and when people will meet, and to contact and involve other people during the meeting ("hey Abby, Tim and I are here and want to know what you think about…"). An interesting point they make is that mobiles are adjusting our ideas of lateness – that it is increasingly OK to be late as long as you are in contact. Of course the unlucky person waiting has their phone with them to call others, and give themselves something to do. "Social voids and waiting times have been filled with contact and coordination via mobile messaging". Ito and Okabe's research also highlights the use of the phone after the meeting – for instance sending texts in dead time on the way home. "What is unique to mobile text chat, however, is that it is particularly amenable to filling even small 'communication voids', gaps in the day where one is not making interpersonal contact with others…". Text chat also has the advantage that it can accommodate itself to interruptions such as getting on a bus or answering a teacher.

The gift of sight?

Bounding over the horizon, video phones have arrived like an excitable puppy. Enabled by more powerful handsets and the technology of sending information as small packets of data rather than one lumpy stream (the acronym is GPRS), and of course the infamous 3G (third generation) promise of greater bandwidth. What effect do these have?

We need to distinguish between two uses. Videocalling, as the name suggests, involves people talking while they can see each other too. The other use there is no clear category title for, but includes recording video (using the camera), playing it back, or downloading and viewing video from other places – such as the news for instance. This turns your phone – theoretically at least – into a sort of glorified video Walkman that you can use to capture your own content too. I was sceptical about video on phones, but have recently viewed high quality TV transmission broadcast direct to mobile, and now think it could be very big indeed.[35] However once you begin to think about the realities of Videocalling (person to person) it all looks a bit

---

[34] In "Mobile E-mail" available at www.itofisher.com/mito/mobileemail.pdf

[35] Stuck on a bus trying to get to the pub to watch a rugby game with friends (I missed all but the last 5 minutes), I'd have happily paid to watch the match on my handset. We all have our trigger point…

less compelling.

Designers often refers to "form factors". What they mean by this are the basic constraints of a device that are at best, tough to escape from, however much you might want to. These need to be taken into account. For instance a door handle needs to be hand shaped and fixed to the door: that's why they are not very good at doing other things too like being a toaster.

The form factors of current mobile devices have some pretty severe limitations when it comes to video calls. For starters how do I hold the phone? The natural position might be in front of me roughly at waist or tummy height. This is where people usually position the mobile for another use where they wish to see the screen: texting, either reading or composing. But from this angle my interlocutor is going to see right up my nose, which (trust me on this) I really don't want them to do. So the obvious alternative is to hold it up at face height which gets uncomfortable after a while, and feels very unnatural. Try it. You can rest your elbow on your midriff or angle your head down, but both seem to me to be awkward work rounds to the essential form factor problem.

Lying down definitely eliminates the problem, and probably has a niche market among the terminally lovelorn, and lazy teenagers unable to get out of bed. Equally I could prop up the phone somewhere convenient, but this destroys the essential element of spontaneity that is part of the appeal of mobile devices.

Assuming I am wrong, and that video calling on phones does become popular, what will this do to our private/public space notions? Can I talk in public over a videophone to someone else? What kind of public space? Could this be a group activity? Most of all, what happens to the sound – is it broadcast to the people near me who are not engaged in the conversation? Perhaps the solution is earpieces: though given their benefits with ordinary voice based calls (your hands are free to do other things[36]) it is surprising that these are not already seen in use more often. The point is, if successful, videophones will exacerbate all the distraction issues we see now.

Distraction and addiction are closely related: substance abuse is frequently a way in which individuals try to prevent reality from impinging too much on their lives. So perhaps a news item in the Independent on 6th October 2003 should not be too much of a surprise.

"More people are becoming addicted to text messaging as a way of escaping problems with face to face relationships, specialists said yesterday. The Priory Hospital in Roehampton, South West London, famous for treating celebrities with alcohol and drug problems, has widened its range of treatment programmes to deal with increasingly complicated addictions. Dr Mark Collins, head of the Priory's addictions unit, said text addicts were just one example of how addiction patterns

---

[36] though not of course with a video call, unless you have balanced the phone somewhere

Mark Curtis

had changed in recent years. The increased role of mobile phones and Internet technology in our ever more stressful lives has bred a range of new behavioural addictions. "The main thing is about avoiding reality and living in an artificial reality" he said".

Digital distraction is enabled by an infinity of possibilities. At any given moment I can call or text the hundred or so contacts on my phone, e-mail thousands of strangers, contribute to a discussion forum, find out about whooper swan migration, check a share price, research a new idea for this book, get a match report from the Spanish second division, read what other people thought of the CD I've just bought. And so on, stretching over entire days and weeks of marginal thoughts explored and links followed without ever doing more than skimming lightly over the surface. Without the discipline to make considered selections, one can gain very little and lose a lot of that most precious commodity, time. Paradoxically all the while feeling busy, busy, busy – and of course connected.

Mountain rescue teams in England have mixed feelings about mobiles: sure, they can save lives in an emergency, but misuse is a real problem according to mountain rescuer Stuart Hulse of the Lake District quoted in the Times[37]. It's a good example of distraction technology at work.

"The mountain rescuers were scrambled and located them within 20 minutes. It transpired that, although the group had gone slightly out of their way, they had no transport and wanted to be driven back to their accommodation. "It would have cost them a fortune to get three taxis to take them all back to their base," says Hulse. "So we ferried them back over the passes." Mountain rescue today, he adds angrily, is increasingly becoming a "nannying and taxi service".

Like many mountain rescuers, Hulse is in no doubt where the root of this problem lies. Mobile phones. Already considered the scourge of city dwellers, the ubiquitous mobile is now creating havoc in the countryside. It has, he says, created a new breed of climber and fell walker who no longer sees the need to go out equipped with a torch, a compass, a map or even adequate clothing because he knows that help is just a phone call away. Common sense and personal responsibility have been replaced by complacency and the expectation of instant gratification."

I'm a keen mountain walker myself, and purchased a GAMIN GPS device several years ago. It's very useful and certainly helped me out of a sticky spot once in snow and fog up a big hill in Scotland. But I am aware as one friend said to me – "it's no substitute for a map and compass" – which of course don't need batteries, but do require a certain commitment to learning. Indeed there is a pleasure in mastering the skills required for using the tools which the GAMIN somewhat takes away (though I'd prefer a better interface).

---

[37] The Times OnLine January 25th 2005

I heard the sailor Sir Robin Knox-Johnston on the radio recently commenting on the achievement of Ellen MacArthur (fastest solo sail round the world). In the sixties Robin was first to do the feat non-stop. He was asked what differences there were then apart from the boat. There was no satnav, he commented, and he used the same techniques that Captain Cook had. He was also asked if he would have liked to be in contact via mobile phone, as Ellen was, in order to feel less lonely. Good god no he replied – half the point of being there in the ocean was solitude. I'm not quoting this with approval in a kind of wistful "those were the days" reverie, just reporting a considered alternative view on the value of technologies we begin to take for granted.

The media are distracted too

There are two sides to the coin of over-communication. One is the personal distraction that I have documented as being a considerable downside of "always on".

The other is that as our media has proliferated it has become both saturated with detail, and unremittingly self referential. Close analysis of minutiae and their meaning shoves aside the big picture. In the late summer and early autumn of 2003 the British media became transfixed by the Hutton enquiry into the tragic apparent suicide of government weapons expert Dr David Kelly. Day after day coverage filled the papers and airtime. A typical day's coverage in the Times and the Independent was on Tuesday 23rd September. The previous day Defence Secretary Geoff Hoon and infamous government "spinmeister" Alistair Campbell appeared before the inquiry for the second time. Both papers covered the day's proceedings with most of the front pages, two special pages inside and leader columns. This would be unremarkable if it was not for the fact that this was typical of the space given to the event since the beginning of the Hutton enquiry on the 11th August.

The coverage on this particular day focussed on extracts from Campbell's diary. As is usual now the arguments turned on textual analysis of a very detailed nature and who said what to whom in efforts to manage the "story" with the press. Naturally the papers revelled in it: stories of spin make the press part of the narrative, and reflects well on its central role in society.

At its heart the Hutton enquiry was about the decision to take Britain to war: but surface detail soon obscured the central meaning until the detail of who spun who became the only meaning most members of the public could take out of it.

Does this matter? It certainly does, because a breakdown of trust is the result. No-one "won" from Hutton – a defining event in the UK in the early 2000's. Central institutions of civil society (the government, the security forces, the BBC) were portrayed – probably rightly – in a highly unflattering light of manipulation, distortion and dissembling. I am certainly not arguing that the Hutton enquiry should not have taken place but the big picture question (should we have gone to war?) was lost in the detail. And the effect was to further cement the idea that presentation matters more than substance.

In the same week speculation over footballer David Beckham's marriage entered the public domain – was it surviving the move to Madrid? The coverage had obviously reached such a level of intensity that the Beckham's were forced into a "statement" to the media. There were no problems. According to the BBC

"Victoria and David Beckham have issued a joint statement denying reports their marriage is in trouble since his move to Real Madrid." The couple insisted they were "extremely happy together" in a bid to end rumours that life in Spain was putting pressure on their relationship. "Contrary to newspaper reports our marriage is not in crisis," they said in a statement released through their management team. "We are extremely happy together as a family. Our only difficulty has been finding a house in Madrid that meets our needs.""

Yet this was not good enough for some. Sunday media speculation immediately claimed that the denial was itself proof that something was wrong. Think about this. If they had not issued a denial, could that not also have been interpreted as evidence of marital discord?[38] Either way, the media wins and the story is again about presentation and analysis of that presentation not reality. In the same year, an ex-children's TV presenter – John Leslie – was accused of sexual assault. After months of frenzied coverage, the implication behind which was clearly that he was guilty, he was acquitted. Without pausing for breath the media switched the story to "my year of hell". All news is good news when you're a tabloid. Lead singer of REM Michael Stipe was rumoured to have AIDs, and that his slender shape was proof of it. When it was not denied by Stipe, it became a "fact". Except it wasn't true.

The media is especially distracted by itself. Here's a challenge – take any newspaper and circle the number of news items referring to other media, their personalities and views. Or assess coverage of any particular major news story: half the analysis will be devoted to what the other media are saying, or how they are being manipulated. The Independent, one of the most serious papers in the UK which takes a principled stand on avoiding coverage of the Royal Family, is not above this. A randomly selected issue had major news space devoted to:

- the story that a website had been closed for naming football players accused of rape
- the fact that the BBC had axed EastEnders from its US channel
- the replacement of venerable breakfast DJ Chris Tarrant at London's Capital Radio with Johnny Vaughan
- the fact that the Oscar judges will not be allowed to preview films on DVD under new rules

---

[38] The fact that it later emerged there probably was grounds for the story is not the issue.

How many of these really count as news? A glance at any of the British tabloids reveals an even more self referential stance. It's media masturbation. We watch the media tell us about the media. This matters because the sheer volume of information and content available to us makes selection very hard: how do I know what to believe? How do I find the stuff that cuts through? Later we will see how faith in the media is declining, and ask if digital can help us find new sources of authority to make sense of the world.

Distraction Crash?

Where is Distraction taking us? In a discussion on this topic Andrew Curry of (future forecasters) Henley Centre commented to me – "Your instinct that it is not sustainable is probably right, but the shape of the crash is hard to see."

The crash is a social one. Distraction media and technologies are creating a dysfunctional society. This trend started with television and has accelerated as we have layered on the "empowering" communications media of the Internet, mobile phones and most recently iPods. Noise cancelling earphones in conjunction with my iPod allow me to cancel out an element of my surroundings – in particular the jet noise on board the flights I often have to take to Helsinki and back. They also do a great job of blocking out the horrendous screeching noise familiar to users of the Victoria Line tube in London. When I get to Brixton, I keep them on, and the music going, and it muffles the touts aggressively marketing tickets to that night's gig at the Academy, it drowns out the drug dealers offering their wares and mutes the slightly deranged bible thumper selling salvation. All of which makes life a bit less tense.... though I realise others might like those cultural inputs. But if I keep them in, what else might be blocked? Birdsong? Casual and friendly encounters? Someone once taught me that one should always ask, what can be learnt from this meeting? What has this person to tell me? We should be questioning barriers to social learning.

It is tempting to take a black and white view. But I am emphatically not doing that. There are many blessings that come with digital communications. It's good for parents to know where their children are because they have a mobile phone, and for those children to be able to call for help if they need it. It's wonderful that the Internet allows us to read, at first hand and uncensored, the views of ordinary people in Iraq even as our leaders unleash war on them. The court of global public opinion now has a medium where it can debate, listen and learn. Smaller things also can make a big difference: like tracking other reader's lists of favourite music on Amazon to discover new sounds you might never have heard. Digital photography is a gift for the cack-handed amateur who can take many more pictures for no extra cost to find the gems, and learn from the feedback they get through the LCD display on the back of the camera.

My friend and colleague Mike Beeston drew an analogy with cars. He likes the fact that he can go and see his parents whenever he wants. His children can go to a school many miles away with relative ease. It's easier to bring the shopping home for sure. Yet he knows there are considerable downsides too. To name a few…cars bring violent death and injury to motorists, passengers, cyclists, pedestrians and wildlife. Swathes of our countryside are buried under unforgiving tarmac. Exhaust fumes contribute hugely to global warming. Urban planning favours traffic flow over community space. For most people cars are neither unambiguously good, or bad. Nevertheless many would also agree with the proposition that as the number of cars per head grows, some kinds of restrictions do need to be placed on their usage.[39]

Should we put controls on the usage of communications? If that sounds far fetched, consider a world where there were no speed limits on cars, no seat belts, no MOT's or car insurance, and unfettered private road construction. It would surely be hell. At some stage society collectively agreed that controls would have to be put on car usage for the good of society as a whole. Few quibble with these, even though they do constrain our "freedom" to go as fast as we like with dodgy brakes.

So if it's not unthinkable to place restraints on the way we use a technology, why does it seem so wrong to consider controls over distraction technology?

Because it smacks rightly of totalitarianism and such a precedent could be abused.

Because from a national perspective our international competitiveness may be affected. Britain is really awfully good at communication. Our language – and our facility with it – is a national asset in an era when English is the international language of communication technology. Our ad. agencies are often regarded as the most creative in the world (well, they say so). Vodafone is the world's largest mobile operator. Everyone admires the BBC except the incumbent government of the UK.

Artificially restraining our exuberance for communication could turn us into the international equivalent of the kid at school whose parents DID NOT LET HIM WATCH TELLY. Every school has one.

Most of all, any legislative attempt to curb distraction would almost certainly be unworkable (how do you ban texts between children after ten at night?) and therefore a bad law.

If legislation is not the answer, what is? The only viable answer is to rework the social contracts which underpin our lives, as the impact of distraction technology becomes clear. What might this look like?

---

[39] A report in USA Today in March 2005 claimed that children in America spend about 6.5 hours a day watching TV and consuming other electronic media (including games). They are watching the same amount of TV as in 2000, but adding in newer technology to the mix.

PART ONE
The Social Price Of New Technology

Chapter Five
The Impact of Media on Social Capital

At this stage we need to pause and consider, just how powerful can communications technology and media be in the effect they have on society? Until 10 years ago, television was the dominant distraction technology. Evidence from the US and Bhutan, two very different countries suggests that television has a dramatic effect on society, and not necessarily for the better. Given their ubiquity, we should take the new communications technologies very seriously as agents of social change.

Television

Despite the extraordinary and rapid advances made by the Internet and mobile telephony, television remains the most successful mass medium yet known to man. Yet it has had some powerful, and I believe detrimental effects on society. Perhaps these are hard to see because at its best telly is, well, fun. After a hard day it is just so tempting to throw off your shoes, grab a drink and let the sofa take the tension, while TV takes care of your mind. It certainly doesn't seem evil. How could we think ill of the technology that brought us the Clangers, Miss Piggy and Monty Python?

In 2000 American social theorist Robert Putnam published a remarkable and important book. The "Bowling Alone"[40] of its title refers to the collapse of bowling leagues in towns across America during the last 50 years, but Putnam is only using this as a metaphor for his central theory that social capital has declined drastically in the USA in the same period.

What he means by social capital is the invisible bonds that tie communities together – "the stock of active connections among people: the trust, mutual understanding and shared values and behaviours that bind the members of human networks and communities and make cooperative action possible". Important features of this are *reciprocity* – people doing things for each other, either implicitly or

---

[40] Simon & Schuster

explicitly sure that those favours will one day be returned, and *trust*. Intrinsic to the concept of social capital is the idea that social networks have value in themselves.

Most people who are not diehard misanthropes will recognise the existence of social capital, even if it may be harder to measure than say, physical capital. At a family level it's called doing the washing up without expectation of immediate return. Among neighbours – where it still exists – it may be putting the cat out or watching their house while they are away.

Putnam pulls together an extraordinary array of data to support his theory that social capital is in free fall in the US. He uses indicators such as political participation, membership of clubs, engagement with associations such as the PTA (parent teachers association), church attendance, trade union and professional association membership, social visiting/entertaining at home, family dinners, card playing, charitable giving (measured against real income). In every one the decline is dramatic, statistically proven and clear – and usually starts from the early sixties.

There are contra-indicators: for instance increased membership of non-governmental organisations such as Greenpeace and the American Association of Retired Persons. But it turns out that where the trends are up either there is a generational difference in attitudes (i.e. it's old people who take part) or the demands on participants are characteristically low. Engagement might be represented by an annual donation, the receipt of a newsletter, signing a petition. People are prepared – with their greater disposable income – to join, but not to do.

Overall there is a shift to more temporary communities with less grip or stickiness. Quoted by Putnam, sociologist Morris Janowitz called them "communities of limited liability" – suggesting beautifully how a group sense of responsibility is being eroded. According to Putnam "large groups with local chapters, long histories, multiple objectives and diverse constituencies are being replaced by more evanescent, single-purpose organisations, smaller groups that "reflect the fluidity of our lives by allowing us to bond easily but to break our attachments with equivalent ease""[41].

I'm not aware of any similar study in the UK – but I'd be prepared to bet it would show similar results, allowing for some local quirks. Especially given Putnam's analysis of why this is happening.

He carefully narrows it down to four factors:
- Pressures of time and money
- Suburbanisation, commuting and sprawl
- Electronic entertainment – chiefly TV (most of the statistics he uses are pre-Internet)
- Generational change

---

[41] This last quote from Wuthnow: Sharing the Journey, Free Press.

The last two are interlinked: the younger you are, the more likely you are to be affected by electronic entertainment. He estimates that the combined effect of TV and what he calls the TV generational difference is responsible for maybe 30% of the decline in social capital.

Can TV really have had such an influence? After all, there has been a never-ending debate about screen violence, and we are regularly assured by its champions that it has never been shown that TV makes children, or society at large, more prone to violence.

Putnam's analysis of the role TV has played begins with two generalised observations on the effect of mass media, telecoms and entertainment. The first is the trend to more individualised news and entertainment. Music is a good example: from live concerts, to recorded discs to MP3's we have moved inexorably towards much greater choice determined by the individual at an ever more microscopic level. News web pages can be personalised, satellite subscription packages specified. Secondly there is a distinct shift to personal and private rather than public consumption, from the concert hall to the Apple I-Pod. Television in particular moved has theatrical entertainment into the privacy of our own homes.

Now for the facts.

By 1995 viewing per TV household was more than 50% higher than it had been in the 1950's. The average American watches three to four hours a day – estimates vary. Television took almost 40% of the average American's free time in 1995, an increase of almost $1/3^{rd}$ since 1965. Again – these figures do not take into account the rise of the Internet and there is evidence that TV viewing has declined because of it, since the mid 1990's. However the Internet is still an electronic screen based medium.

Between 1965 and 1995 Americans gained an average of six hours per week in added leisure time, and spent almost all of them watching TV. "Time diaries show that husbands and wives spend three or four times as much time watching TV together as they spend talking to each other, and six to seven times as much as they spend in community activities outside the home."

The amount of television viewing done alone has also risen. "At least half of all Americans usually watch by themselves, one study suggests, while according to another $1/3^{rd}$ of all TV viewing is done alone". Among children the figures are worse. Less than 5% of TV watching is done with their parents.

A very important distinction is between habitual viewing (leaving it on in the background or switching it on just to see what is on) and intentional viewing (switching it on to watch something specific and pre-chosen). One could just as easily call the habitual form distraction viewing. Guess what? Habitual (or distraction viewers) are much less socially engaged. "Selective viewers are 23% more active in grassroots organisations and 33% more likely to attend public meetings than other demographically matched Americans. Habitual viewing is especially detrimental to civic engagement. Indeed the effect of habitual viewing on civic engagement is as great as the effect of simply watching more TV". In case you are thinking, 'well hey its just the Slobs and I'm safely middle class', note the key definer – "demographically matched". In other words this affects all strata of society. Selective viewers, even in the later 1970's outnumbered habitual viewers by more than three to two. This has now been reversed.

Putnam believes that once other factors that might affect civic engagement are accounted for, on average each extra hour of TV viewing per day reduces activism (going to meetings, membership, letter writing) by 10%. He shows clearly that there is a link between the amount you watch TV, and how much you are likely to do for society in general. For instance in one study 39% of light viewers attended a meeting on town or social affairs in the year, compared with 25% of heavy viewers. 29% of light viewers had played a leadership role of some kind in a local organisation, the figure for heavy viewers was 18%.

Just to ram the point home, among this group of well educated working age Americans, there were nearly twice as many heavy viewers. Dependence on TV for entertainment is the "single most important predictor" of civic disengagement.

So what you may be thinking. It is certainly easy to be cynical: at times Putnam comes close to conjuring up a possibly mythical land before the sixties when everyone earnestly helped each other and played together – modern ideas of fun don't seem to enter into it. In British terms, do we really wish to return to a dull but worthy land of boy scouts, Women's Institute jams and Rotarian dinners?

But his social capital is not only about institutions but also about our social connectedness. "People who say that TV is their 'primary form of entertainment' volunteer and work on community projects less often, attend fewer dinner parties and fewer club meetings, spend less time visiting friends, entertain at home less, picnic less, are less interested in politics, give blood less often, write friends less regularly, make fewer long distance phone calls, send fewer greetings cards and less e-mail, and express more road rage than *demographically matched* (my italics) people who differ only in saying that TV is not their primary form of entertainment." I know which club I want to be in.

Of course this does not on its own prove that TV is the culprit. It is certainly associated in some way with the decline of social capital – could it be the cause, or an effect? It's hard to be sure but here are some pointers.

All the indicators for civic disengagement begin to flicker alarmingly in the 1960's about ten years after the widespread availability of television – i.e.; just as the first TV generation began to hit the workforce and make an impact (or not) on society.

Mark Curtis

Canadian researchers in the early 1970's found a trio of remote towns, one of which (they christened it Notel) had no television, sited as it was in a wrinkle of the landscape. As TV arrived here, they compared levels of civic engagement using the two other similar towns which already had TV as control cases. They concluded that there was a direct link between TV and a lessening of social ties. Studies in other countries have had similar results.

Paradise Lost?

But the most dramatic evidence to support Putnam's theory has come since he wrote Bowling Alone. Tragically it is emerging from the most unlikely place – Bhutan, the most remote country in the Himalayas. Television was illegal and unknown in Bhutan until 1999, when the Dragon King allowed it in as part of an ambitious modernisation programme. There are now 46 cable channels, chiefly provided by Star TV. There are also now rising problems with violence, fraud, drugs – even murder. This in a traditionally Buddhist land. In a brilliant and disturbing article in the Guardian, in June 2003 Cathy Scott-Clark and Adrian Levy explored what was happening. It's worth quoting extracts at length because the article illustrates a number of themes of this book, besides pointing a finger compellingly at TV as a social disruptor.

"April 2002 was a turbulent month for the people of Bhutan. One of the remotest nations in the world, perched high in the snowlines of the Himalayas, suffered a crime wave…

The Bhutanese had always been proud of their incorruptible officials – until Parop Tshering, the 42-year-old chief accountant of the State Trading Corporation, was charged on April 5 with embezzling 4.5m ngultrums (£70,000). Every aspect of Bhutanese life is steeped in Himalayan Buddhism, and yet on April 13 the Royal Bhutan police began searching the provincial town of Mongar for thieves who had vandalised and robbed three of the country's most ancient stupas. Three days later in Thimphu, Bhutan's sedate capital, where overindulgence in rice wine had been the only social vice, Dorje, a 37-year-old truck driver, bludgeoned his wife to death after she discovered he was addicted to heroin. In Bhutan, family welfare has always come first; then, on April 28, Sonam, a 42-year-old farmer, drove his terrified in-laws off a cliff in a drunken rage, killing his niece and injuring his sister ..

…But none of these developments (schools, hospitals, roads), it seems, has made such a fundamental impact on Bhutanese life as TV. Since the April 2002 crime wave, the national newspaper, Kuensel, has called for the censoring of television (some have even suggested that foreign broadcasters, such as Star TV, be banned altogether). An editorial warns: "We are seeing for the first time broken families, school dropouts and other negative youth crimes. We are beginning to see crime associated with drug users all over the world – shoplifting, burglary and violence."

Every week, the letters page carries columns of worried correspondence: "Dear Editor, TV is very bad for our country... it controls our minds... and makes [us] crazy. The enemy is right here with us in our own living room. People behave like the actors, and are now anxious, greedy and discontent."

But is television really destroying this last refuge for Himalayan Buddhism, the preserve of tens of thousands of ancient books and a lifestyle that China has already obliterated over the border in Tibet?...The Bhutanese government itself says that it is too early to decide. Only Sangay Ngedup, minister for health and education, will concede that there is a gulf opening up between old Bhutan and the new: "Until recently, we shied away from killing insects, and yet now we Bhutanese are asked to watch people on TV blowing heads off with shotguns. Will we now be blowing each other's heads off?"

...Downtown, at the southern end of Norzin Lam high street, a wriggling crowd of children press their faces to a shop window. Inside the headquarters of Sigma Cable, the walls are papered with an X-Files calendar and posters for an HBO show called Hollywood Beauties. Beneath a portrait of the Dragon King, the in-store TV shows wrestling before BeastMaster comes on. A man in tigerskin trunks has trained his marmosets to infiltrate the palace of a barbarian king. When the monarch is decapitated and gore slip-slaps across the screen, the children watching outside screech with glee. Inside the Sigma office, the staff are scrapping over the remote control, channel-hopping, mixing messages. President Bush in a 10-gallon hat welcomes Jiang Zemin to Texas. Midgets wrestle on Star World. Female skaters cat-fight on Rollerball.

...The marijuana that flourishes like a weed in every Bhutanese hedgerow was only ever used to feed pigs before the advent of TV, but police have arrested hundreds for smoking it in recent years. Six employees of the Bank of Bhutan have been sentenced for siphoning off 2.4m ngultrums (£40,000). Six weeks before we arrived, 18 people were jailed after a gang of drunken boys broke into houses to steal foreign currency and a 21-inch television set. During the holy Bishwa Karma Puja celebrations, a man was stabbed in the stomach in a fight over alcohol. A middle-class Thimphu boy is serving a sentence after putting on a bandanna and shooting up the ceiling of a local bar with his dad's new gun. Police can barely control the fights at the new hip-hop night on Saturdays.

...While the government delays, an independent group of Bhutanese academics has carried out its own impact study and found that cable television has caused "dramatic changes" to society, being responsible for increasing crime, corruption, an uncontrolled desire for western products, and changing attitudes to love and relationships. Dorji Penjore, one of the researchers involved in the study, says: "Even

Mark Curtis

my children are changing. They are fighting in the playground, imitating techniques they see on World Wrestling Federation."

...Sangay Ngedup is one of the only government ministers willing to voice concerns about television. For the first time, he says, children are confiding in their teachers of feeling manic, envious and stressed. Boys have been caught mugging for cash. A girl was discovered prostituting herself for pocket money in a hotel in the southern town of Phuents-holing. "We have had to send teachers to Canada to be trained as professional counsellors," says Sangay Ngedup. This march is not just against a sedentary lifestyle; it is a protest against the values of the cable channels. One child's placard proclaims, "Use dope, no hope." "Breast is best," a girl shouts. "Enjoy the gift of sex with condoms," reads a toddler's T-shirt.

...How quickly their ancient culture is being supplanted by a mish-mash of alien ideas, while their parents loiter for hours at a time in the Welcome Guest House, farmers with their new socks embossed with Fila logos, all glued to David Beckham on Manchester United TV. A local official tells us that in one village so many farmers were watching television that an entire crop failed. It is not just a sedentary lifestyle this official is afraid of. Here, in the Welcome Guest House, farmers' wives ogle adverts for a Mercedes that would cost more than a lifetime's wages. Furniture "you've always desired", accessories "you have always wanted", shoes "you've always dreamed of" – the messages from cable's sponsors come every five minutes, and the audience watching them grows by the day.

...Bhutan's isolation has made the impact of television all the clearer, even if the government chooses to ignore it. Consider the results of the unofficial impact study. One third of girls now want to look more American (whiter skin, blond hair). A similar proportion have new approaches to relationships (boyfriends not husbands, sex not marriage). More than 35% of parents prefer to watch TV than talk to their children. Almost 50% of the children watch for up to 12 hours a day. Is this how we came to live in our Big Brother society, mesmerised by the fate of minor celebrities fighting in the jungle?

Everyone is as yet too polite to say it, but, like all of us, the Dragon King underestimated the power of TV, perceiving it as a benign and controllable force, allowing it free rein, believing that his kingdom's culture was strong enough to resist its messages. But television is a portal, and in Bhutan it is systematically replacing one culture with another, skewing the notion of Gross National Happiness, persuading a nation of novice Buddhist consumers to become preoccupied with themselves, rather than searching for their self."

The Bhutan story is compelling evidence that TV can be a startlingly powerful force for change, and not necessarily positive, in society. "Young people are now much more in tune with what is happening around the world" Shocksan Peck who has studied the influence of television in her country, told the BBC. "The more we learn about the world, the more we lose our own culture"[42]. We can see how it operates as a distraction technology in many ways; as parents favour it over communication with their children, the same children want to look more American, farmers desire fast cars. Context goes missing (how much do the Manchester United channel viewers really know of the Stretford End?) It's easy to ignore this in the west. Or take the view that it's patronising to tell other societies how they should be. We've all grown up with broadcast media and the idea that it affects us one way or another is not new. Robert Putnam has shown that (in conjunction with other factors) it tears at the social fabric, and that from the introduction of a medium the effects of this disruption can take 10 years to become manifest. But the underlying deep changes – the Bowling Alone of his title – may not become clear and explicit for another 30 years. Putnam wrote his first article on this theme in 1995. In Bhutan it appears to be happening faster – perhaps it is a special case, because the change is accelerated and exaggerated by the extreme difference with what went before.

We need to understand how television does this. Overall it is clear that it competes for scarce time. Are there other psychological effects more inherent in the medium or its programme content? Culled from a number of sources, Putnam shows that:

- TV viewing is habit forming, leading to dependence
- Heavy TV viewers suffer disproportionately from headaches, indigestion and sleeplessness
- TV allows social connections to be divorced from reality and creates a false sense of companionship
- TV gives people the sense of engagement without effort i.e.: without actually being engaged
- TV encourages us to attribute problems to individuals rather than society

"TV privileges personalities over issues and communities of interest over communities of place. In sum TV viewing may be so strongly linked to civic disengagement because of the psychological impact of the medium itself". Hauntingly, he concludes his assessment of the impact of mass media with the image of 21st century bowling lanes, mounted by giant TV screens. The bowlers are still there as in the 1950's, but conversation is stifled, by the moving images that absorb them as they await their turn. It is not a uniquely US phenomenon. Walk into a British pub and see the drinkers distracted by Sky on a big screen.[43]

---

[42] Quoted in the Independent, 18 June 2004

[43] Before I sound too much like a killjoy, I should concede that there is a flip side, and watching big football and rugby games in pubs is a new form of social congregation which has brought pleasure to many, including myself.

As we become conditioned to the new media and the era of world wide instant communication, so some disturbing effects are clear. Those who *create* news are beginning to realise that they have to compete for attention with *everyone* else. 9/11, live on TV around the globe, was an epochal moment. Now extremists on one side capture our attention by releasing video of a hostage having his head sawn off. On the other side in the same conflict, and in a private capacity, soldiers have sex in front of prisoners and video the event. The more we see this kind of thing, the more it is normalised.

A recent film – Bus 174 – documents the sad events of a June day in 2000 in Rio de Janeiro when a young man took an entire bus hostage. The drama was played out live on TV for four and a half hours. Brazil stopped to watch it. Speaking on a radio interview, the director of the film, Jose Padhila, observed that Sandro, the street kid in question, appeared to *perform* once he realised he was on camera. He was in his own movie, and reacted as you would if you are conforming to dramatic stereotypes imbided since birth.

TV is a distraction technology. We cannot assume that the newer digital media and mobile telecoms will bring with them no social change, or that if they do, it will be only positive. We must begin to engage with the likely distraction effects of digital media, and bring into the public sphere a discourse that seeks to understand cause and effect, and shape our usage of technology accordingly.

We have seen how the impact of one medium on society can be intense and un-planned for. We also need to examine whether we can continue to live comfortably with the growing volume of communication across all media.

PART ONE
The Social Price Of New Technology

Chapter Six
Sustainable Communication?

Can we have too much communication? This chapter looks at the issue. Is it possible for us to deal with the amount of messages we receive and send out, without sacrificing some other activities such as thought? Spam is a clear sign that the opportunities afforded by digital for more and better communication can easily be subverted to more and worse. We can also see that we are all spammers now, and organisations are struggling to deal elegantly with the consequences. It leads in fact directly to a worsening of service.

In the personal sphere, it is also ironic that ease of communication seems in many cases to be endangering relationships, as we look at evidence that the new technologies make a range of illicit behaviours easier than ever before. And even sleep is under subtle attack.

It's good to talk?

Sustainable communication sounds suspiciously like two buzz words, awkwardly coupled together like trains from a different railway gauge.

Sustainable is a word we are hearing a great deal of now. What does it mean? According to Fritjof Capra[44], the concept was introduced in the1980's by Lester Brown, founder of the Worldwatch Institute. He defined a sustainable society as one that is able to satisfy its needs without diminishing the chances of later generations. In other words, we should not take out of life more than we put back in. Global warming, the eradication of species, loss of bio-diversity – all these indicators are telling us that we are living unsustainably on our planet. This basic model is being applied to many areas of life: business, architecture, farming and fishing to name the most prominent.

Can it apply to communications too? To be fair – it sounds initially like a stretch.

---

[44] "The Hidden Connections" Harper Collins

I thought of making it the title of this book, but after a discussion with friends and colleagues, abandoned this notion on the basis that the word is both over-used and poorly understood.

However, it is a useful approach to consider modern communication and technology through the lens of sustainability. Firstly because it is a model that is being used more and more across society for evaluating our actions and their consequences. The communications industry (in its widest sense including IT, media, telecoms and marketing) will become seriously out of step if it does not align thinking with trends elsewhere.

Secondly because asking some questions – like what kinds of communication may be unsustainable, and why, may generate insights and answers we need to take on board.

Litter louts exist on line too

Not surprisingly spam is the first candidate for consideration.

I have an e-mail address I use for everything that isn't work or friends. It's on Hotmail, and I give it out to all kinds of organisations via paper forms and on web sites. In the last few years, like many other people, I have been deluged with spam. In a typical 24 hours the following arrives unsolicited in my inbox (among some stuff I did want).

Kara promises me three inches more and 30% extra width. Aimee offers a brunette teen str!pping down (note the use of the exclamation to avoid spam filters). Julian.n.chad says I can lose weight in the shower! Apparently it involves cider which sounds fun but unbelievable. No more feelings of embarrassment (sic) tempts me with increasing my bra cup size. Ted has Viagra for sale. Walter Williams writes from Nigeria to offer me the opportunity to have $35m US transferred into my bank account: all I have to do is give him the details! Ask Us How To offers increased energy, weight loss, reduced wrinkles, And Much More!

This is pretty typical. Sadly for the purveyors of these delights, I'm interested in buying none of them, though it might be fun to try Viagra one day (but not from Ted I think). Their business models are very sustainable – it costs next to nothing to send an e-mail, and the abundance of spam suggests that it works for certain categories of product and service: specifically sex, pharmaceuticals, personal health issues such as dieting, conmen and financial services (some of these vendors may be the same organisations).

In a paper – "Spam The Current State" – published in August 2003 Andrew Leung of Telus Corporation offers an excellent analysis. According to Andrew approximately 40% of all e-mail on the Internet is spam. It's growing too – spam was up fivefold over the previous 18 months. The reasons are not hard to see: it's

Mark Curtis

easy and cheap to set up and run (you only need a PC and an Internet connection). Spammers only get a response rate of 0.005%: that is 50 out of one million people, but they can make money on less than that so cheap is it to buy lists. Leung quotes a price of $150 for 70 million e-mail addresses on a CD. With the 1 in 20000 response rate quoted above that's 3,500 new suckers. If the product in question costs $50 (the youth elixir I was offered today came in at that price per bottle), that is revenue of $175,000. Assuming a profit margin of 40%, the spammer makes $70,000. Not bad for $150 and a few key strokes.

Spammers are very sophisticated, and I don't mean that they read Proust in the original or know whether '99 or 2000 is a better year for Burgundy. Among their tactics they "harvest" e-mail addresses with programs which bombard Internet service providers (for instance AOL or Hotmail) with guessed e-mail addresses like **mark.curtis63@xyz.com**. A response is added to their database. The cost of doing this declines all the time.

Spam, as many people are now discovering, has also come to mobiles. A friend went on a train journey recently. Short of things to occupy his mind, he entered a competition on a can of Pepsi. As is now standard with on-pack sales promotions run by products with a youth bias, the entry mechanic involved mobile texting. On the face of it, this is more fun for the consumer (instant no hassle entry). And it is much better for the promoting company. Not only does someone get to keep a percentage of the margin generated by the text (often the sales promotion agency), but now they know your number too and have a mainline into your life.

This particular competition offered Tom – my friend – the "opportunity" to win one of 400 places at a Miss Dynamite concert. When they asked him his age (42) it became apparent to him that he was unlikely to be a winner of the big ticket item. So it proved. Still, he did get the consolation prize of a ringtone delivered to his phone, seconds later. Actually he lost the ringtone when he tried to save it – which is probably a good thing as I doubt Miss Dynamite would have gone down well at the very straight oil company he works at.

A couple of days later, he got an unrequested text offering him the opportunity to meet "young singles" in his area. Now because Tom only uses his mobile for work, and has never given out the number to any source outside friends and colleagues, he thinks the Pepsi promotion is the source of the leak. He can't be sure, and probably will never know. It seems unlikely that Pepsi would have sold his details to a dating company, but perhaps there were other agents in the chain who were less scrupulous.

At its wildest fringes this is not a nice business. Here's another typical, and real, message received unsolicited.

"From: URGENT! Your Mobile No. was awarded £1500 Bonus Caller Prize on 1/8/03. This is our final try to contact U! Call from Landline 090 6636 9547

BOX97LDNW7QP, 150PPM"

Notice the sting in the tail: following an apparently meaningless series of numbers and letters is 150PPM, which translates as £1.50 per minute. In other words, we will keep you on line for as long as we can and that'll be £15 if we get you to 10 minutes. The numbers in this business are interesting – it probably cost 6p to send that text. If only 1 in a 100 people respond, and stay on line for 5 minutes, then total cost = £6, total revenue = £7.5. So someone makes a profit of £1.50 per 100 sent out (not including any other costs and maybe the occasional prize). Which is only £7500 for every 500,000 numbers. But telephone number lists are more expensive than their e-mail equivalents. So you wonder if it is worth the game – or if response rates are actually much higher than 1%. Perhaps some other scam is in there too to fleece those truly dumb enough to persist on the line. It also seems sadly probable that those least likely to be able to afford the calls will be the most likely to respond, like lottery tickets.

So right now there seem to be two prevalent mobile spam models offering either sex or free prizes (surely someone will combine both shortly). There are also two big problems with this: intrusion, and suggestion – or the digital honey trap.

The mobile phone is the most personal technology device yet invented. That's why the ringtone and icon business has exploded: these ultra cheap downloadables let consumers customise their phones to tell the world who they are in a pathetic squeaky sort of way. So spam on a phone is even *more* intrusive than in your e-mail inbox. For a lot of people, a text arriving is an event (who is it? what's inside?), which reinforces their sense of identity (someone wants me). It's more than a little disappointing to discover that you're wanted by some scuzzball with a nice line in scam.

Tom is happily married and has deleted the text. Nonetheless, how many people, in or out of relationships, respond to the suggestive type of message? Someone out there wants you! Here's the highway to find them!…(at 25p or more per text). Suggestive on its own is fine and is all around us in the media. But on phones and in e-mail the sheer level of repetition undoubtedly tempts in a way that humans have not been exposed to before.

Spam Reversal

In an ironic twist, the very organisations who have over-used communications technology in the past are now struggling to cope with the volume of incoming fire.

Seventeen years ago I applied for my first mortgage. Working at the time in Soho, my first port of call was my bank branch on Oxford Street, London. I had to fix an interview with the manager. He wore a suit and so did I. I went in as a supplicant and probably sat with hands folded on my lap. Everything was going swimmingly until I

Mark Curtis

revealed that I was about to become a father. His face went grim. I got a lecture on the unlikelihood of mothers returning to work, no matter what they might say before the baby arrived. As our income base had just irretrievably halved in his view, we could not have the mortgage. In Thatcher's Britain it was critical to get your feet on a rung of the property ladder. It was not the brightest moment of my life.

I'm sure banks still refuse mortgages. But many other aspects of the experience would be unrecognisable to today's 25 year old. Especially the notion that you should go somewhere and talk to someone. It may not even be clear who you should talk to. It's a better world in some ways: there is much fiercer competition to lend money and many more ways to find and secure a good deal, especially through web intermediaries. Money Supermarket will show you pages of deals from different suppliers with just a few clicks.

Going to a branch was a much more considered process. It took time to get there, nerve to sit in front of the manager, thought to communicate what you wanted. You did not do this easily or lightly. You also generally only got one choice of product. But it cost the banks time too, so they wanted to deal with you more efficiently and technology – initially the telephone – offered an attractive route.

In striving to make the process more convenient for customers, and "efficient" (read lower cost) for themselves, the financial services providers inadvertently reduced the amount of consideration required by a customer before they made contact. They are now having massive difficulty dealing with the consequences.

Steve Lloyd of Logica CMG, an IT company which (among other things) helps banks figure out what to do about it, says it is going to get worse as the generation accustomed to texting spontaneously become customers. Already the number of calls and e-mails are spiralling out of control with no extra business resulting. A typical bank may get 2.5 million phone calls a month, compared with pretty much none in the 1980's except local branch traffic. It's like reverse spam.

What do you do with spam? You filter it. This is exactly what the new breed of automated phone systems (also known as IVR) are designed to do. The companies that use these are well aware that they drive customers mad (welcome to Deafco! In order for us to be able to handle your call better, please listen to your choices – if you are enquiring about sales please press 1, etc…) They know they lose calls while you go into the endless loop of being told what a valuable customer you are, but are prepared to pay the price if they can fend off "valuable" customers with a touchtone response. According to Steve, one well known telecoms company in the UK forces customers to go through 70 key impressions on their phone just to top up a pay as you go account.

My colleague Olof and his girlfriend recently moved house. They needed to interact with the gas utility, a broadband provider, a mortgage company, two kinds of insurance company (buildings and contents), the water utility, a new gym, and lawyers. Not one of them provided a satisfactory experience, which is unsurprising but if you think about it a shocking statistic. He says that they now trust organisations to get things wrong, not right.

What has changed here is the nature of conversation. Actually it barely passes muster as a dialogue. The process has been chunked down to bits, bytes and grunts. Using the Internet you can launch multiple enquiries and focus them precisely – just tell me your interest rate – without engaging in a full discussion.

It makes it very hard for a company to have a single view of you, the customer, if you persist in sending signals via phone, branch, ATM, mobile, web, interactive TV and post. The holy grail of customer relationship management (CRM) is known as the single customer view. This is where every single bit of the company knows all the things about you that the other bits know. But very few organisations have achieved this, and meanwhile they continue to throw money at CRM software "solutions". Sadly the aim of (the very misnamed) CRM is to enable the organisation to "cross sell" (persuade you to buy insurance when you have a bank account) or "upsell" (persuade you to spend more on the same service). Would you want a "relationship" with someone who is always and only intent on cross or up selling you? Somebody will eventually make a fortune persuading companies to reverse the whole idea: that software should allow the customer to manage the relationship to their satisfaction, not the other way round.

Commercial conversations have become fragmented, by time and channels. This is both a symptom and a cause of a decline in trust. For many people, perhaps like me with a legacy of patronising bank manager stories, the boot is now on the other foot. They don't trust companies not to rip them off, and therefore don't want a conversational relationship. Yet the more companies also fend them off, unable to cope with the volume of fragmented enquiries, the less time trust has to develop through conversation.

Once again we see that digital is stripping out context. Transactions are stripped down to their raw components, and what is lost is mutual understanding. As usual we are both winners and losers. Consumers are "empowered" – to use the current terminology – with greater choice. But try telling that to the punter who has been hanging on the telephone for 30 minutes trying to navigate a "self-help" maze.

Eventually of course, many people do get through to call centres. Is it so surprising then that the other biggest problem organisations face apart from soaring numbers of calls, is high staff turn over in call centres? In some it is reported to be over 30% per annum, with all the entailed costs of training new staff and de-commissioning leavers. Overall numbers are huge: a UK bank may have over 8,000 call centre staff. Demoralised agents, often recruited in geographical areas where wage costs are low, struggle to field efficiently (often irate) customers with a wide variety of questions, and a different context behind each and every call. The latest trend is to shift call centres to developing countries…I'd love to know how they impart the context of the bloke in Acacia Avenue, Warrington to staff in Bangalore. But staff attrition (as it is charmingly called) is up to 25% already in India.

Yet quite reasonably, don't you expect an organisation to remember what you've told them before? And do they? This may be the most infuriating aspect of all – the apparent lack of listening.[45] It's a skill which forms 50% of a good conversation. Without it we are just voices, yelling in the wilderness. In the digital age, companies need to learn not just to listen attentively, but demonstrate that they have too.

Is this picture of a world of spam and fragmented conversations sustainable? On three counts it is not. Firstly the Internet and mobile phones have brought with them many benefits to mankind. But spam devalues communication through these channels. It takes longer to find things that are relevant. The messages themselves become less compelling, and the important ones tainted by association with dodgy hair replacement therapy. Bit by bit, the barriers go up. So if the result is that we use the technologies less for the things they are good for, we all lose. Leung makes the point repeatedly that "marketers are not aware of the social or real total costs of their actions. Due to their nonchalant attitude, they will reply to any consumer complaints by repeating the same mantra: "If you don't like an e-mail, just delete it"".

Secondly spam imposes expenses – chiefly in lost time – on individuals and business. In January 2003 Yahoo reported an estimate for this as $13.4 billion for US and European businesses. Other analyses quoted by Leung suggest a figure of €10 billion for Europe alone.

The UK government has just banned spam. It's a good and needed step, undermined by the fact that most spam comes from outside the UK.

It's harder to know what legislation can prevent the third sustainability issue: that the on-line environment is increasingly being blamed for the break-up of relationships. Divorce Online[46] reports that half of all divorce petitions it processes involve Internet adultery and cybersex behaviour. Relate claim that 10% of couples that seek its help cite the Internet as the third party causing problems. I went to Divorce Online (a "self help and information service for England and Wales"), and entered the key words "cybersex" into the search engine (I had picked up the story elsewhere and was looking for the source). The results of the search – presented on Divorce Online itself were, with supreme irony:

1. Cybersex: UK's most extreme HARDCORE – no credit cards – click here!
2. The biggest cybersex site: the world's hottest porn site featuring etc…
3. Cybersex – UK only! Etc…

---

[45] Olof's comment was that this lay at the heart of his negative house move experiences.
[46] www.divorce-online.co.uk

Scrolling down the page I found the news article I had come for. Of course I'm not suggesting that this web site deliberately lists porn sites among self help tips on divorce. I'm sure they have very good legal advice. Their search engine just dumbly returns what it finds across the Internet.

Quoted in the Register[47], J Lindsey Short Jr of the American Academy of Matrimonial Lawyers said: "the computer is a great communications device. But spouses need to remember to communicate with each other as well…While I don't think you can say that the Internet is causing more divorces, it does make it easier to engage in the sort of behaviours that traditionally lead to divorce."

Perhaps because mobiles are less prevalent in the US than Europe, Mr Short sticks with the PC. But in Italy they have adopted cell phones with gusto, for all areas of their life. The BBC reported[48] that "a new survey published by Italy's largest private investigation company says that in nearly 90% of cases, it is the mobile phone that reveals or betrays extra marital activities…Beatrice Ruggiero, a divorce lawyer in Rome, says…"I've noticed perhaps 30% more divorces in September and October than last year…and lots of my clients are saying they discovered their partner's infidelities during the summer holidays because of SMS messages sent on mobiles". Apparently one of the mobile phone operators is planning to introduce a dual sim card, which would have the effect of making discovery harder. One Italian private investigator has published 'The Five Golden Rules' on how to not get found out.

While it is charmingly Italian to focus on the problems of discovery, the issue would not arise if the mobile did not lend itself so well to creating the problems in the first place. Of course infidelity existed long before digital technology. But as American lawyers and Italian private eyes know, it makes it a lot easier.

Even divorce has been carried out by text. An Islamic court in Malaysia has approved a divorce that had been notified to one half of the couple via SMS. After a quarrel, the husband sent the following text, "If you do not leave your parents' house, you will be divorced." Gulf News has reported that SMS messages have been cited as reasons for divorce in at least 15 other cases. Malaysia's civil government is in the process of banning divorce via text message.

There is a serious question here: are we happy to continue to facilitate communications structures which undermine relationships so easily?

Someone is out there 4 you

Of course, not all digital flirting is adulterous or damaging.

The dating market has seen tremendous growth since the Internet took off in

---

[47] www.theregister.com 11 September 2003
[48] www.bbc.co.uk/news 15 September 2003

Mark Curtis

the early 1990's. Even before then the dating market has always been a big market because dating is an essential part of our lifestyles & will always be.

On-line (web-based) dating is a big winner of the last few years.

- In spring 2001 a Canadian report backed by msn and written by academics from the university of Toronto found that 1.1 – 1.2 million Canadians had visited an on-line dating site, and the potential for online dating services was a further 2.5 to 2.8 million adults (this was dating not flirting). This equates roughly to a 19% of adult population market size
- They saw 4 forces driving this:
  - a growing proportion of the population composed of singles
  - career and time pressures increasing, so people look for more efficient ways of finding partners
  - single people more mobile because of job marketplace changes, so harder to find partners
  - workplace romance on decline because of sexual harassment sensitivities, also online dating "seems to be safer than conventional dating"

According to comScore Media Metrix, more than 45 million Americans visited online dating sites in May 2003, up from about 35 million in December 2002. The Online Publishers Association projected that spending on Internet dating sites in 2003 would be $100 million or more per quarter, compared to less than $10 million a quarter at the beginning of 2001. The New York Times is forecasting a $400 million market for online personals in 2004.

The OPA/comScore Networks report claims that individuals who pay for personals content are likely to spend both more time and more money online. Whereas the average Internet user spent 6,143 minutes online and $83 in e-commerce purchases during the first quarter of 2003, the average personals content purchaser racked up 13,895 minutes and $238.72 online.

Meetic a French company is active in France, Italy, Spain, Germany, Great-Britain and Belgium and has already "seduced" 1.5 million web users. Datingdirect.com in the UK claims over a million users.

Flirting is already a prime use of SMS.

Although the above statement is known anecdotally, figures are now beginning to back it up.

- Over 2/3rds of European phone users regularly use SMS (Forrester Research)

- Dutch SMS traffic went up by 45% on Valentine's day in 2002 (Europmedia.net)
- 24% of Europeans claim to have engaged in "txt sex" (Phillips)
- Germans and British are most likely to send romantic messages.
- Italians and Spanish are most likely to use phone for love affairs.
- In Asia half of mobile phone owners feel it is easier to SMS somebody they are attracted to than to actually speak to them (Siemens)

Recent surveys now show that mobile dating services in South Korea (a large mobile data market) have seen very strong growth in the last few months. Specific mobile dating services are now growing – mainly based on sms or wap. Taiwanese cellco Far EasTone claims that one of the most successful applications on its multi-media portal, Bravo, is a dating game in which players interact via avatars. Almost 30% of the carrier's active GPRS users subscribe to the service, says FET president Jan Nilsson. Track Ur Mate has become the most profitable value-added service of leading Indian carrier Airtel. It has 65,000 paid requests per day, according to Sandy Argawal, Landmat's Asia-Pacific managing director.

Match.com, went mobile with AT&T Wireless in 1Q02. Anecdotally take-up figures began to rise in June, when MMS was incorporated into the service, enabling users to message photos of each other. AT&T Wireless will confirm the claims, but say the service is "doing very well."

Meanwhile one service (for the terminally insecure) has sprung up on the web offering software which tracks if the e-mail you sent has been opened, how long it remained open for, if it was reopened and forwarded.[49]

Behind all of these examples drawn from different corners of the communications world, we have to ask is it sustainable to be "always on?". The answer already looks a lot like no. On the 17 September 2003 the on-line IT newsletter the Register gave the headline "Mobile phones disrupt teenagers sleep". A lot of teenagers leave their phone on at night. The details came as no surprise – a study conducted by the University of Leuven in Belgium, published in the Journal of Sleep Research, claims that the noise of text messages arriving in the middle of the night was affecting the sleep quality of almost half 16 year olds. Presumably these messages are coming from other teenagers who have also been woken up by the siren bleep of incoming SMS, in a kind of viral consecutive disruption. Even among 13 year olds the figures for woken over once a week were over 13%.

I know its true because, with two teenage daughters, I've heard it happening, and been woken by it too. Interestingly the howls of protest when as a parent you suggest that mobiles are switched off at bedtime are rooted in their concept of

---

[49] DidTheyReadIt.com

Mark Curtis

"rights". It's their right to be always on, apparently. But when it messes with their ability to function as amiable humans the next day, I'd suggest something unsustainable is going on.

It is well documented that business people have discovered something similar in the last 10 years. Technology brings the office to them, and if they are unfortunate enough to be workaholic (unable to place their private life first) then e-mail and mobiles are first rate tools for prioritising the company. It's a relationship killer, and for many people therefore unsustainable.

A reasonable counter-argument to this is that it is the choice of the individual to use technology in the way they see fit. Just because you have sharp knives in the kitchen does not mean you are going to stab yourself with them. This is the "technology is neutral" standpoint. It *may* be in intent, but is often not in consequence. Sometimes it is not even so in intent: a handgun has only one real end use in mind – to shoot other human beings, hardly the hallmark of a morally neutral device.

The expectations of our peers and reinforcement by the media of what constitutes behaviour to aspire to, mean that we do not operate entirely in a world of free will. That is not an excuse for abuse, merely an observation that we have to address the issues of unsustainable communications, which literally ruin lives.

Return to this question posed at the beginning – can we have too much communication? Surely we have been encouraged to believe, that that the more we talk, the better the world will be? But it seems to me that this is based on the face to face model. If we follow the path of increased distraction over 5, 10, 50, 100 years, where will it take us? What will evolve? How will we adapt? Answers to these questions are likely to be largely wrong, because we cannot escape the context of now and truly see what standing in the future looks like. We might usefully ask instead, are we equipped to deal with the new levels of communication? This question in turn leads us to examine our use of time.

PART ONE
The Social Price Of New Technology

Chapter Six
The Time Paradox

Even if it was possible for our brains to deal with the volume of information emerging from our use of distraction technology, the time available to us in any one day is still fixed. Many observers believe that lack of time is now the central daily concern of humans. This chapter looks at the connection between time and the new world of communications. It goes on to examine how a reliance on mediated communication may run the risk of isolating us from experiences and interaction in the 'real' world.

Pretty much everything you might desire can be acquired, used and enjoyed faster now than thirty years ago. Immediacy is a defining feature of our culture. This is a long term social trend, closely entwined with the rise of consumerism post second world war. Digital communications further facilitate it, Examples include the shift from theatre, to film, to TV, to video, to DVD and TIVO. At each stage we dramatically reduce the time taken to get what we want.

Ironically a price (not the only one[50]) we pay for immediacy is loss of "free" time. This is because managing the technology itself (learning and relearning the hardware and software, frequent upgrades, dealing with theft, insurance etc..) usually requires lots of effort. This is called by one observer "consumption work". It's on the rise – it can also be recognised in the way companies now try to "outsource" work to customers. The best known example is automated caller systems, and there are plenty of places where it happens (the government is doing it too!). Time has become a battleground between organisations and their customers.

In our efforts to create more time for ourselves, mankind inexorably creates products and services out of activities once done without money changing hands. New technology is increasing the potential for this to happen to areas of life previ-

---

[50] We also lose the sense of occasion or event. It's not a hard choice to pause a DVD to get up and make a cup of tea – but leaving the cinema half way through a film to go to the loo is a wrench precisely because you can't stop the film. This creates a sense of tension, in itself dramatic.

---

ously untouched. As usual, the upshot will be neither good nor bad – but we need to engage with what it might mean, especially if it distances us from experience.

Have it now culture

Waiting is not very fashionable. We are awfully impatient now. Our relationship to food provides great evidence that this is so. Airfreighting around the world and production under plastic mean that we no longer have to wait for fruit until the local season is in – it's strawberries all year round. Supermarkets are open 24 hours a day. We can buy fish at three in the morning and on Sunday too. "Fast" food is a massive industry in its own right. Pre-prepared meals are marketed on speed of cooking as well as convenience. Microwaves get us closer to the consumer nirvana of "instant".

We can see the same trends in media. Live performance, with its implicit anticipation of event, of fixed time and place, of potential mishap or of never to be repeated excellence, still exists. Alongside it (and more popular measured by usage) we have broadcast, recording and playback and network technologies. All of them without exception have tended towards immediacy in the last 100 years, and at a faster rate in the last 10. The news used to come to town by messenger. Fire beacons could send simple news (invasion!) more quickly. The Royal Navy used flags to signal complex news from Portsmouth to London in Nelson's time. All this was considerably speeded up by telegraphy, radio, the telephone, television. The reality of the Vietnam war shocked America partly because TV images arrived so soon after the events they brutally laid bare. The first Gulf war gripped a global audience in real time, likewise the infamous events in New York of 11th September 2001. Now SMS text alerts follow us around to tell us what is happening wherever we may be. Mobile communications are once again a big shift forward here, because we no longer have to wait to pick up information or communication: it comes to us wherever we are.

Perhaps in our love affair with immediacy we are also seeing the decline of the long term project, though whether that is cause or effect is beyond this author to know. Society as a whole seems unable to grasp the ecological issues surrounding global warming, partly because the solutions required are long term, the effects distant beyond our lifetimes. Governments acquiesce and are complicit in short termism. Rising divorce rates testify to an inability to commit to long term projects for life.

We even look for short term solutions for our bodies. The popular response to weight problems is diet. The quicker it works the better – diet solutions are sold on speed. There is an even more rapid and radical response: have it sucked out! Liposuction literally removes unwanted fat from parts of the body in a stream of liquefied lard. Wouldn't exercise be a better and more natural treatment? The trouble is that as a course of action exercise leaves a lot to be desired: it's hard work, requires a consistent commitment, can be unsociable, and worst of all takes too long.

Author Susan Greenfield sees big problems ahead for a mankind that prefers short term pleasure to longer term striving. She explicitly links this to technology, as I am seeking to do, and her concern is focussed on the brain. Greenfield (a neuroscientist) singles out education as an area of concern and asks if "an emphasis on interactivity would blur the distinction between the new tendency for a visceral, immediate response and a thought-out opinion"[51]. She imagines that the "children of the future no longer need a long attention span to follow a linear narrative of words but rather are trapped in the immediacy of the 'now' – ever-stronger flashing lights and bleeps may be needed to sustain motivation or concentration over time frames of seconds". It is now known that the cognitive part of our brains responds to stimulation by growing the all important neuronal links, but only if the input is sustained and focussed. She worries that the pattern of connections in our brains may literally become less complex and therefore less powerful if we accept too much experience though technology, filtered and selected for immediate satisfaction. Another term is sensory overload. " …the basis of pure pleasure is a configuration of the brain such that the active contribution of the personalized connections – the mind – is temporarily non-operational. Small children, lacking extensive connections anyway, are more easily the passive recipients of their sensory input, having a 'sensational' time. Adults, however, turn to extreme measures: drugs that blunt the functioning of our neuronal connections, or such rapid, successive input though our senses from, say, fast paced sport, that no single connection has time to grow before it is displaced by the start of another. Be it wine, women or song, or the modern analogue, drugs and sex and rock'n'roll, there is a strong premium on sensory, non-associative input; in all cases our brains revert to a simpler, sparser pattern of connections, we recapitulate the 'booming, buzzing confusion' of the infant brain. This state of sensory oblivion, stripped of all cognitive content and bereft of self-consciousness, is probably more like the consciousness that most animals experience most of the time. It is to this hedonistic, passive state that the new technologies could be taking us, a state that we enjoy, but that up until now has only been temporary. By incessantly stimulating neuronal connections into highly constrained configurations, the new technologies might jeopardise the very existence of human nature, permanently."

So four troubling questions need to be asked and answered.

- Will technology mediated immediacy reduce our mental capacity and sense of self?

---

[51] The quotes from Greenfield are all from "Tomorrows People", Penguin Allen Lane

- If we live for the moment, will we build and leave behind anything of value to society?
- What is truly special in a world where you can have most of what you want, instantly?
- And, the Dalai Lama has wondered, if our tolerance for delay goes down, do we then have less space to love those who cause delay in our lives?

Definitive answers only lie ahead, but it is in our power to grapple with these issues now.

Things get more complex, not less

The culture of immediacy has driven manufacturers to exploit technology which facilitates it. One of the big success stories of the digital era is the digital camera. In the space of about six years it has become the image making weapon of choice for most photographers. Even the professionals now use them. In theory, the shift from film based to digital photography is very empowering for anybody who takes, and enjoys looking at, pictures. The list of benefits is impressive. You no longer have to:

- visit the chemist or a high street developer when you wish to process pictures
- pay extra to see them
- wait to see them
- buy film
- worry about where the negatives are

And in addition you can now store all your pictures in a tiny space (your hard drive), arrange them into multiple albums, search for them easily and change their appearance.

So in theory, a move to digital photography should make pictures cheaper, more fun and accessible.

The reality is not so simple, and variations of what I am about to describe will be familiar to many.

Compared with the old fashioned routine of giving your roll of film to a developer, there is a lot more you have to *do* to enjoy digital pictures. For starters you have to find a way to get the pictures off the camera on to a PC (assuming that is the tool you will use for storing and printing). If you're lucky, you can plug and play (i.e.: the pc will recognise the camera when you plug it in). If like me, your first digital camera was given the cold shoulder by your computer, you have to invest in

Mark Curtis

a small device just for transfer which can "read" the memory card or storage media which usually replaces film on a digital camera. This costs about £50 more. You plug it into the computer, and then you can transfer the pictures. So very quickly the new camera owner comes up against the issue of **compatibility**.

Next up as an issue is **storage** space. Naturally you very rapidly fill the original storage card you bought with the camera. So you invest in more cards (because theoretically it costs nothing to take and process a picture you find you are taking many more). I used to take around 100 pictures on a summer holiday – now I come back with maybe 250 and will have deleted many on the trip to free up room on the memory cards. The cards have got cheaper: a 64 megabyte card which can store roughly 80 good resolution pictures costs about £20. That is certainly cheaper than film when you consider it is reusable until you scratch it, lose it or upgrade your camera (more of this in a moment). Of course I'm not going to store the pictures forever on the memory cards (that *would* be more expensive shot for shot than film). So at some stage storage becomes an issue for your PC as you transfer the pictures.

Initially this certainly is no problem. But then you have to start organising a filing system for them. Each set of pictures will typically be numbered something like 001.jpg or 025.jpg. Each new set you download has the same numbering! So you have to keep them in different folders because the computer cannot cope with the fact that they have the same file names. Gradually you evolve a naming system for the folders which allows you to find stuff reasonably fast – monikers you can understand like "July 2003" or "Pamplona" or "Chris". However even in a folder with a helpful name such as "Honey's first steps" it is hard to distinguish between 004.jpg and 044.jpg, unless you open them and have a look. Which takes time, because most people's PC's still don't render memory hungry pictures that quickly.

Help is at hand. There are now some really good photo album software packages, which allow you to **organise**, view and play with your pictures much more easily. I've been using one called iPhoto from Apple for three years now, and it's well designed. I can create albums, play slideshows, edit pictures (rotate, crop etc..) and many other tasks too. For instance you can name each picture, and give it a rating of one to five stars.

But when I reached about 2500 photos (trust me it happens) I noticed that the software started slowing up considerably. It became frustratingly hard to scroll through the pictures, even in thumbnail mode, at anything faster than a dozy snail pace. When this happens, all the other benefits begin to fade into the background, and the thought occurs that it would be quicker to flick through an old album.

Apple aren't stupid, so they upgraded iPhoto recently and completely solved the problem, which is good because I've got over 4000 snaps on there now. However, in order to run the new software I found I needed to upgrade my system! Which cost more money and, importantly, time.

With 4000 pictures of my life all in one place my next concern is **backing** them up – or making sure there are digital copies somewhere else in case my computer is lost or destroyed or seizes up. I can burn them to a CD, but unfortunately no single CD will hold the more than 1GB of my very important memories. So now I've had to buy an external hard drive, and copy to that from time to time. When I remember.

Printing at home seems like a good idea too. But what a lot of people don't seem to realise is that it isn't cheaper. The paper alone costs between £4.50 and £5.50 for a pack of 20 standard photo size leaves. Replacement colour cartridges for a cheap (sub £100) printer cost at least £18, I've no idea how long these last but my printer appears to eat them like Scooby snacks. Ofoto, the Kodak on-line print service charges 24p per print at the same size – so even including p&p, home printing is probably twice as expensive. So it's still better (measured by cost) to send off for photos after all.

Then we had a burglary. Our new computer will not acknowledge the old card reader! So I had to visit the web site of the device manufacturer to download the "driver" software which allows the computer to see the device, which reads the card which has the pictures I took on my camera (in the house that jack built), Except the device company has been swallowed by another company who no longer sup-port "older" devices by making the drivers to work on newer computers. So now I have to figure out a new way to get the pictures off the camera. Those at ease with technology are probably reading this and shaking their heads, bemused that I did not pursue easier or more obvious (to them) fixes. But I suspect that to the ordinary user, my story is not unusual.

Eating Time

It's not at all clear that digital photography is cheaper, given its reliance on periph-erals and other kit (a PC, back-up space, smart cards, print paper, ink cartridges). However the bigger theme running through this is time. The true price we pay for the all the cool stuff we can do with digital is the amount of extra time it takes to do everything. Again I must stress that I wouldn't go back to film, and really enjoy using iPhoto. But the benefits don't come as cheap as we think. Here are some of the ways in which time can get swallowed up:

Mark Curtis

Digital photography	Old style photography
Downloading pictures from camera to PC	Taking the film to the shop
Sorting the pictures into albums	Picking it up
Naming the pictures	Being annoyed at the number of poor pictures you've taken
Rating the pictures	Putting them in an album or a shoebox
Deleting unwanted pictures	
Editing (improving) the pictures	
Sending them to be printed	
Working out how the software works on camera and PC	
Backing up the pictures	
Working out how to transfer the pictures onto a new computer when you upgrade that	
Getting all the software to work together	
Downloading upgrades to the software	

There has been a great deal of debate over use of time in the modern world. About ten years ago a phrase emerged to describe the condition: "time poor". We ask how it is that we seem to suffer from more stress related illness than ever before, and yet statistically it is by no means clear that individuals are working harder. In addition, we have an abundance of labour saving devices compared to our ancestors. However it's a consistent feature of sociological studies of the last 20 years that westerners complain of their lack of time.

But according to one survey[52] free time in the USA has increased from 35 hours in 1965 to 40. Between 1995 and 2001 working time decreased in every country in Europe bar Denmark, Sweden and Finland.[53] However it is clear that leisure time is more spread out, that work invades the weekend and "leisure just doesn't feel like leisure".[54] Being always on in the mobile age surely doesn't help.

---

[52] Quoted by Greenfield, carried out by Penn State University
[53] Labour Force Survey/nVision quoted in "Complicated Lives", Willmott and Nelson, (Wiley)
[54] Greenfield

In "The Making of a Cybertariat", author Ursula Hews explains the paradox. Industrial societies have tended to take tasks that were previously done in the home "for free", and turned them into profitable business or (less often) state run institutions. Areas affected include preparing and preserving food, nursing, washing (clothes), cleaning, fire making, making clothes, caring for the sick and elderly. In other words previously someone (usually women) scrubbed, wrung, dried, weaved, peeled, chopped and comforted. Now we rely much more on machines to wash clothes bought from the Gap, microwaves to heat ready made meals, TV's to provide companionship for elderly relatives and the young. Like Hews I do not wish to romanticise life in a mythical time now distant, which was in fact often brutish, smelly and short. Yet "one very interesting aspect of this socialisation of housework has been that it has not reduced the total amount of time spent on it, as one would logically expect it to. Although new opportunities have been created outside the home for paid labour, the amount of unpaid labour inside the home has remained more or less constant with, if anything, a slight increase."

Why is this? Hews points to a rise in what she calls "consumption work". Although new devices and businesses save us time – and a washing machine definitely does make washing easier – other manifestations of our complex consumption patterns chew through our "leisure". Examples include:

Consumption work	Problem	Examples
Buying	Choosing the right product or service at the right price	• Which computer? MAC or PC? How soon will it be made redundant by new products?
Training	Understanding how a device works	• Learning to drive • Reading a manual
Running (day to day)	Other raw materials need to keep service going	• Fuel and oil for car • Detergent and conditioner for washing machine • Detergent AND salt AND rinse aid for dishwasher • Emptying the Hoover
Maintenance (occasional)	Legislation and by products of consumption Fault diagnosis	• MOT AND insurance AND road tax for cars • Hoover goes wrong, reread the manual (if you can find it), take it the retailer, call manufacturer helpcentre etc....
Consequences	One thing leads to another	• Easier washing encourages us to wear more clothes which leads to more washing

Mark Curtis

To add to this, there is a very clear trend for organisations to "outsource" work to customers whenever they can. Although we now hear a lot about outsourcing to other countries (i.e.: getting workers on the Indian subcontinent to do jobs at a fraction of the cost of Europeans and Americans), this was preceded by the realisation that costs could be saved by getting the buyer to do as much of the work as possible. Maybe the supermarket was the first manifestation of this (you collect, sort, weigh and price the goods). Of course big consumer benefits came too – choice, freedom to browse and select, a greater variety of goods. Other examples of the outsourcing of consumption work have much less clear advantages for the user – for instance corporate touch tone call answering systems, self service petrol, self assembly flat pack furniture (arrgh), having to buy a ticket from a machine *before* you get on the bus (now the case in central London). The government are doing it too – the best example being the shift to annual tax self assessment. No longer does the Revenue tell you how much you owe, you have to figure it out and tell them!

So things that were previously done for free are now paid for, and some costs such as storage, transport and selection have been successfully transferred to buyers. This helps to explain why during the 20th century time spent on "housework" has gone up not down. Other causes that Hews lists include advertising which forces up the standards and range of housework (it's important to kill all known germs dead, as Domestos ads tautologically tell us), more smaller scale households (less people in each to do the work), and new types of household consumption activity (mowing the lawn).

Hews again; "It is possible to view economic history as a history of progressive commodification. By this I mean the slow transformation of activities carried out for simple use or for exchange outside the money economy into activities carried out for monetary gain." This process spins out yet more activity and associated products and services and expert support. "The inexorable drive towards the creation of more and more "products" is therefore closely associated with the creation of new forms of "consumption work" and on the other with a growth of "service work"." These are another place where our time is disappearing.

Hands off?

There is definitely a distancing effect here. Because we think they save us time (and effort) we use machines, and mechanisation places us at one remove (at least) from the action. A friend of mine recently did some work with a well known UK food company: the marketing team he worked with were genuinely stunned to learn that he and his wife prepare all their food fresh, every night. Pre-packaged utility is now the norm, not the exception. We are machine operators, not hands-on doers. Does this bring more satisfaction? It certainly brings more frustration when things go wrong and we have to call in the experts. At these moments our loss of direct control becomes very evident in stress.

"In the first stages, this externalisation (of labour) is often welcomed by consumers, who feel empowered by it. Faced with waiting in a long line to buy a railway ticket, investigate the availability of a library book, fill a car with gas, or have the vegetables weighed and labelled, most people prefer to do it themselves, even if this means grappling with an unfamiliar user interface. Problems start arising when there is no longer a choice: when the alternative of being served by a human being has been eliminated, and the individual is left to encounter the ATM machine, the self service ticket machine or the unattended gas pump alone". In these cases the time saving machine has had the reverse of its intended effect.

It's easy to overdo this. A faulty petrol pump that doesn't kick into operation when you shove it in the car is hardly a show stopper. Mature grown ups should be able to deal with such things without registering as blips on a sociological stress meter. Most of us would much rather face these problems than diptheria, choking smog, high infant mortality, rampant damp and other truly unpleasant conditions largely consigned to history books in developed countries.

Some things do disappear, like those on the list above. Most remain. Futurologists like to make predictions of replacement. They see something new coming, and foresee that it will replace what has gone before. But on-line banking has not eliminated bank branches (though along with many others I thought it would) – both co-exist. Video did not destroy cinema. Homeworking is rising, offices remain. Generally the effects of innovation are not OR but AND. The result is MORE, and therefore increased choices to make, added complexity, greater distraction as we ponder what to do, how to do it. On their own each extra manual to read or interface to master is insignificant. What is of concern is the gradual accumulation of stuff. It means more time to be spent dealing with it.

If this theory (the commoditisation of private work) can seem overly focussed on laundry issues, consider sport. Sport was initially games played between individuals or teams of amateurs. It often still is. It has also become very big business. What was initially a social and free pleasure on parkland became part of the money economy at the most skilled level. The effect is visible back in the park – recently I saw part of a kids game in my local park. One boy particularly caught my attention: not only because he exhibited eye catching skill but also because he had modelled himself down to the socks on David Beckham, complete with long locks scraped back under an alice band. About 15 yards out he trapped the ball with his back to goal, swivelled and rifled it perfectly into the top right hand corner of the net through a crowded penalty box. It was awesome and he knew it – racing across the pitch pursued by his mates, this ten year-old performed a well choreographed dive with arms spread out (known as a Klinsman after the German who invented the cel-

Mark Curtis

ebration). I suspect it was also the dance of an ambition fed by the comprehensive commercialisation of football. This is not intended to sound like a critical stance: professional sport brings huge enjoyment to participants and fans alike.

The commercialisation of discourse

Might the commoditisation of much that was free, largely in order to free up leisure time (and make money of course), also have a socially distancing effect? I think it was Theodore Zeldin who said that conversation is the basic currency of civilisation. Until the telephone, conversation was more or less free (pubs and coffee houses have historically made money out of being venues for talking). Of course almost all still is free – when carried out face to face. Over any distance beyond shouting reach, telecommunications are now there to assist – and of course we pay for the privilege. This has been the case for more than a century. The difference now is the range of conversational media which have become available. Located firmly in the money economy are instant messaging, e-mail, blogs, sms, mobile phone calls, web site forums, livechat (on web sites and phones), push to talk (a walkie talkie service on mobile phones).[56]

Of course this is not new; it has always been inherently true with the basic telephone that the telco is selling you "content" produced by whoever you are talking to, in this case their voice and words. Our content becomes valuable when connected to other people. But over-reliance on forms of communication which help us talk at a distance may be part of a trend towards second hand living.

Don't get too close to me

At the same time as mankind has striven to move to an on-demand lifestyle, so it has sought to distance itself from experience. Since the beginning of the industrial age, Western culture has been on a relentless path away from direct contact with anything which might be deemed visceral, distasteful or unclean. We saw earlier how labour saving devices frequently have the effect of turning us into machine operators rather than hands on doers. The history of warfare and (again) food in the last three centuries provide striking examples.

Until relatively recently, war was chiefly an affair carried out on foot and horseback. Killing and wounding, essential activity in warfare, were achieved either by hand using swords, pikes, spears, clubs or by projectiles such as arrows, spears

---

[56] In fact in the digital world, the customer's content frequently becomes embedded as an essential part of the product. This is only the start. As we shall see later, we're about to see a new wave of personal content media. They hold out the prospect of new social challenges and benefits.

and rocks. The latter allowed men to project lethal force towards opponents some way from them, or hidden inside fortifications. The advent of gunpowder greatly enhanced a combatant's ability to deliver death at a distance. Cannon and muskets, later rifles and shells, changed the battlefield forever. Increasingly the soldier who pulled the trigger did not witness the result of his action close up. This became marked by the time of the First World War when the majority of fatalities on the Western Front were caused by shellfire. Of course vicious hand to hand fighting still took place, but the overall trend was clearly now away from face to face confrontation and towards remote aggression.

Why was this? After all, the lethal effects of a bullet and a sword aimed well are still exactly that, terminal. The initial advantage of a gun is that the user exposes themselves, theoretically, to less danger. However once armies are similarly equipped, the advantage of superior distance killing disappears, and in fact casualty figures from Waterloo, the American Civil War and the First World War bear this out. Nonetheless it became clear that the human cost of distance destruction (for the sender at least) was lower than direct confrontation, given superior odds. For those on the receiving end, the reverse was true, as the Basques discovered at Guernika in 1937 when the German Condor Legion dispensed bombs from their planes on market day to terrible effect, and invented the next phase of total war. Missiles, bombs delivered by plane, rockets: all project force efficiently. Fewer soldiers are put at risk by their despatch. Sadly many more civilians usually suffer when they arrive.

More recently in Vietnam and the two Gulf conflicts we have seen the very clear reluctance of Western society to stomach combat when it puts their troops at risk – preferring instead the "surgical strike" promised by "intelligent" weapons systems. I am not making a moral comment on this: all death caused by war is to be regretted. But the trend is clear enough – away from direct bodily risk and towards indirect violence. The enthusiasm of medieval warriors or Nelsonian ship boarding parties for high risk, bloody and terrifying combat now seems almost incomprehensible. Another side of this coin is that the attitude towards death of suicide bombers bewilders us.

Our complex relationship to killing extends to food too. Ada, the heroine of the book and film "Cold Mountain"[57] has what seems a very modern, urban sensibility. Left to fend for herself on her deceased father's country property, she is at a loss how to gather food "despite the fullness of the growing season…she was perpetually hungry, having eaten little through the summer but milk, fried eggs, salads, and plates of miniature tomatoes from the untended plants…even butter had proved beyond her means, for the milk she had tried to churn never firmed up beyond the consistency of a runny clabber. She wanted a bowl of chicken and dumplings and

---

[57] Charles Frazier (Sceptre)

Mark Curtis

a peach pie, but had not a clue how one might arrive at them." She is rescued by the arrival of country-wise Ruby who promptly despatches a cockerel that has been tormenting Ada, by pulling its head off. Later they eat it.

Are we all Adas now? Our relationship to food has utterly changed since industrialisation lead to the majority of Europeans and Americans living in towns and cities. It would be interesting to know what proportion of the population in Britain, for instance, has ever killed an animal in order to be able to eat it. Less than 1% I would guess. I wonder how many would be prepared to? Our modern sentiments militate against such a thing. We have become used to meat packaged in such a way as to disguise both its origins and explicit death for our nourishment. Chicken is cut up into easy to cook cuts and comes wrapped hygienically in plastic on a polystyrene platter.

As a young boy I went to Spain for the first time in the early seventies – to a very remote village in Andalucia – and carry strong memories of a food culture that was in stark contrast to suburban London. Chickens bought from the village shop came complete with heads and feet, curled and tucked into comical positions. These had definitely once, and very recently too, been birds. We also noticed that the flavour made British supermarket chicken seem closer to its plastic wrapping than poultry. On a memorable day, my father decided to buy rabbit for the table. He was directed to a near neighbour, an old lady in mourning black who ushered him into her ground floor stable where plenty of rabbits frolicked in the straw. "Which one do you want?" she asked. My father indicated one vaguely. To which she said "well, go ahead". I suspect his hesitation gave the game away and she knew that he had expected her to do the dispatching.

At another time I witnessed a pig killing, carried out by the gipsy butchers in the open square outside the charnel house nestling the end of the church. A river of blood and water washed freely down the central gutter of the steep village streets as they went to work scorching the hairs with flaming brushes of broom, and scalding the skin with boiling water. These are powerful visual memories for me partly because such things are so well hidden from view in a big modern city.

As discussed previously, the big news in food retailing in the last decade has been the rise of pre-prepared meals. Now there are lots of reasons for this to do with microwaves and households where both parents work. However the effect is to distance us even more from production: now the chicken has been boned, sliced and smothered in sauce.

At least in the UK, organic and related movements such as farmers' markets, have recently striven to reconnect consumers with the sources of their food. Abel and Cole, an organic grocery company delivers boxes of seasonal food to the door, complete with a weekly newsletter highlighting the farmers and their methods. Yet farmers complain that consumers are still more sensitive to price than their best intentions would suggest.

Other examples abound of how we have put barriers and technology between ourselves and the world. The captain of a sailing ship had to be an expert in navigation, the complex interplay of sail,wind and rope, ballast, and leadership. Steam took away the requirement for many of his skills – discussing the likely advance of powered vessels, fictional naval captain Jack Aubrey complains in 1812 in the novel "The Fortune of War"[58] of "the probability that sailors should soon have to turn into vile mechanics". Travel by car, train or aeroplane insulates us increasingly from the "outside". Edward Tenner[59] points out how quills had to be sharpened and dipped in ink until the steel nib came along. Then replaceable cartridges removed the need for ink bottles, and in turn these have largely been replaced by disposable pens. The blue/black mucky stuff has been contained. Birth is called labour for a reason, it is extremely hard – but drugs are increasingly being used to lessen, even distance the impact and elective caesarean section is undergoing a marked rise. We prefer to exercise in the gym rather than run in the wild (we actually pay to take away the wind and rain!).

Digital technology can distance us from the world, because as we have seen it affords multiple new opportunities to immerse ourselves in representations rather than the world itself. Swiss author Max Frisch said that technology is "the knack of arranging the world so that we do not have to experience it". But we learn and grow through experience and interaction. The second half of this book examines how we can use the new media to these ends.

---

[58] Patrick O'Brian (Harper Collins)
[59] "Why Things Bite Back" (Fourth Estate)

PART TWO

The Social Potential
Of New Technology

PART TWO
The Social Potential Of New Technology

Chapter Eight
Deep Media

This chapter proposes that digital media could be more enjoyable and easier to use. In order to create communications which touch us more deeply, I propose a series of "rules" called "deep media". My aim is to challenge both creators and consumers to think harder about the content new technologies deliver to us with such facility.

We look at why the rules are required, and why the time is right now. The suggestion is that deep media can be achieved through greater storytelling, more humanity, better context, the use of body language, sticking to established and useful conventions and simplicity.

Insanely great?

Much of the new media is ugly. A fair amount is wearisomely hard to use. A great deal of the content is superficial, marooned in a sea of its own limited understanding, with no meaningful relationship to anything else. How many "insanely great"[60] web sites can you think of? Places where content, function, interaction and aesthetics combine to create a truly memorable experience? Now try the same exercise with say films, or books, or TV programmes. With a little thought, the average person may well be able to name twenty to thirty films that he or she is passionate about. For each of these other media it is much much easier to think of (many more) wholly engaging creations than it is with the web.

In fact I suspect that if you were to carry out the exercise across the UK in 2004, the same web sites would consistently float to the top – the BBC, Amazon, eBay. Great web sites, largely characterised by superb functionality, content and interaction design – but hardly memorable for their aesthetics. Other digital media – PC software, mobile phones, interactive TV are worse. With the honourable exception of Apple, most software is unappealing to look at or engage with. The first iteration

---

[60] The title of a book by Stephen Levy which eulogised the Apple Macintosh

of WAP or mobile Internet browsing has been widely perceived as a failure for a wide range of reasons, among which was that it simply looked awful. The next generation of WAP browsing is still aesthetically challenged. No-one I know has ever raved about something they did or saw on Interactive TV.

This is not good enough. Despite the billions spent on digital media since 1993, the user experience is often poor, rarely amazing. It is time to begin to push the boundaries of our expectations and reach for the gorgeous. How to do it? Numerous conversations I had with colleagues at Razorfish between 1999 and 2001 (when it was already clear this was an issue) produced a set of ideas called **"deep media"**. OK – jargon alarms will now be going off in reader's heads but I hope to prove that this is a useful wrapper for a bundle of thoughts, some common sense, some provocative. I should also say that the term is intended mainly for use with the new digital media, not older technologies, like film, analog TV or newspapers.

What does deep media mean? In truth it's a mindset, a way of thinking, perhaps best summarised as "try to put humanity back into technology where it's missing". Some principles follow – though we should be naturally suspicious of anything that looks like design rules. Deep media is a refusal to accept the status quo. The principles – such as they are – have three audiences. The first is the designers who can apply them each and every time they invent, improve or develop a product or service. The second is those content and media owners (this includes individuals pursuing personal publishing) who in effect "own" or at least are responsible for the digital artefacts the rest of us consume. And the third is of course everyone who consumes digital media. By demanding depth the latter group can be very influential.

The following are the key guidelines that are intended to deliver deep media:

* Introduce storytelling wherever possible
* Create beauty, apply humour, be playful
* Reveal context
* Design "body language" into the experience
* Respect design conventions that make it easy for people
* Simplify all the time

We'll look at each one in depth ;-) in a moment. I'm sure there are other approaches – these ones happen to have been tested on many people through everyday work in the last five years at Razorfish and Fjord, and have been met globally with recognition as genuine needs. None of these elements are new, most are applied with patchy frequency and effect already. But there remains so much room for improvement that a call to arms is required.

There is a problem with the list which should be signalled now – and designers reading this will have immediately noticed it. The last two principles are in direct tension with the other four. How can one say, in effect, 'make it easy for users', and in the same breath insist on more confusing detail through narrative, fancy design and what appears to be a generalised demand for lots of extra stuff? Doesn't this introduce complexity, one of the things that this book believes is distracting us?

Done poorly, it will. Design which hides function beneath creative decoration is useless. Yet a tension between usability, functions and aesthetics can be a source of creative inspiration from which great products come. There are also grounds for optimism that deep media can be both easier to use, and more fulfilling (in many ways those statements go together anyway as good designers know). Firstly the time is nearly right to do this; broadband uptake is rising, giving more people access to faster data via their PC's and mobiles. Richer interfaces may be within our reach without having to wait an age to see them. Secondly examples of deep media are out there. Thirdly we have learnt a great deal from the last 10 years of digital media. Some of the lessons are beginning to be evident in design – web sites are becoming better. Fourthly, if we challenge design to give us what we want, we may get it. But only if those who pay for design give them permission to create magic.[61] So the fifth reason for optimism is that in the relentless search for competitive advantage, product and service owners may just be beginning to realise that brilliant experiences give them the edge in a crowded environment. The evidence for this lies in our experience over the last year with clients and the mood of the market for design in general.

Deep media is **not** the same as rich media. Rich media is a term usually used to signify a general increase in the use of animation, sound and especially video. It is applied to content on both web sites and mobile phones. Rich media is certainly increasing: the mobile operator Three is partly betting its future on rich media on phones becoming very popular. But adding audio and motion does not necessarily give added beauty, context or sense of story and identity. More is required. The ancient medium of books prove that depth is different from richness: a good novel, printed in black and white, is not rich media (though it surely is in our head), but does have depth and resonance. In fact an over-reliance on rich media may be an issue for traditional content owners who tend to believe that what works in one medium will work in another. You can't just put TV on the web, a book on the TV, a film on a mobile. Big media organisations have discovered that this is the case with the web, but seem to be about to go through the same painful process on mobile phones (where, for example, amplified sound through a speaker is so bad as to be barely an option. So until it gets better, or everyone uses earpieces, audio cannot be relied upon).

---

[61] If this sounds far fetched, the founder of Apple's Human Interface Group, Bruce Tognazzini, wrote a fascinating paper in 1993 on the connection between magic and software interface design which can be found at www.asktog.com/papers/magic.html

Why bother?

Why is deep media needed? From a commercial point of view, we've seen the answer already. It can confer benefits to any organisation that wants to provide its customers with a better experience. These days the sources of sustainable competitive advantage eventually boil down to three: the quality of relationship you have with customers, the culture of the company and a constant programme of innovation. Deep media can improve the first of these, only happens if the second is strong, and is an innovation in itself.

From the point of view of the user of digital technology, a deep media makes more sense of what is experienced, ensures it is more memorable, and provides a higher reward for the commitment of time that media consumption implies. It enhances enjoyment and facilitates choice: in a world full of demands on your attention, this approach helps you decide what to focus on by giving clearer resolution of the whole picture.

Well designed video games give us a peak at deep media in action. There is usually a strong sense of narrative (in fact this element is becoming increasingly important as exemplified by games such as The Getaway which uses the streets of London as the background to a crime story where you are a participant). As graphics cards and processing power improve, so games designers have sought to create lush and immersive worlds for us, though this was already happening more than ten years ago. Anyone who played the classic Myst will understand that beauty was very much part of the game. Interaction with characters provide opportunities for body language: in an early Sonic the Hedgehog the eponymous hero would tap his foot impatiently if you took too much time over a move. Context is provided on many games by shifting camera angle or the ability to view maps, or other parts of the game world. One approach to deep media would be to challenge service providers to make their customer experience more like a game (though not if it irritatingly gets in the way of what users want to do!)

If video games can do it, why to date have other digital media been so poor? The simple answer is that it is too early in the lifecycle of the technologies we are addressing for it to have been any other way until now. Roughly speaking, 1993 – 1996 saw a great deal of experimentation on the Internet. Between 1996 and 1998 the new business models (e.g.: on-line bookstores, portals, search engines, auction sites) began to emerge. From 1998 onwards there was an orgy of investment and some money making until the retreat in 2000 catalysed by the collapse of tech shares on Nasdaq. The retreat lasted until 2003. Meanwhile the 90's witnessed the mass adoption of mobile phones, initially with voice as the "killer app". Just as the web went into reverse, the growing success that has been SMS became clear. But then telecoms dropped out of flavour with the stock market too. Now the market for

Mark Curtis

communications technology is heating up again.

Against this background we should not expect design and content formats to have reached maturity. Perhaps they never will: the history of media is mixed in that respect. The basic format of films has been stable since sound was introduced (about two hours long, projected onto a big screen), with experimentation taking place constantly on the fringe (shorts, animation, epics). On the other hand television has never ceased evolving since it was introduced (think about MTV, breakfast shows, reality TV, rolling news such as CNN). Either way, whether digital media eventually has a mature plane to reach or not, it certainly has a lot further to go. How can we be confident of this? There are three reasons: its relative immaturity, the continuing development of technology and lastly the changing ecology of media.

Expect more change

Digital communication is really only 10 years old (less if you consider mass market adoption as the tipping point).[62] Consider TV from the 1960's (a decade after its mass adoption). Apart from the fact that much of it is black and white, it now looks almost unbearably antiquated (even the colour bits). If it didn't, much of it would be re-used by TV channels. Imagining the perspective of someone twenty years from now, it is hard to believe that the era of experimentation with digital content is over.

Secondly the technology is still advancing. For instance personal video recorders (PVRs, which use digital technology) such as TiVO or Sky Plus are changing viewing habits. By 2006 25m American homes will have these, and already 650,000 UK homes have Sky Plus. Among other benefits, viewers with PVRs can very easily skip advertisements. According to TiVO viewers do this about 60% of the time.[63] Consider what this might do to TV. Advertisers will try to find other ways to reach viewers (for instance sponsorship and product placement), and some of them may abandon the medium altogether. In addition PVRs go hand in hand with electronic programme guides (EPGs). Together these allow you to select content that you want to watch *when* you want to watch it. They also permit content selection in a variety of novel ways – for instance by finding programmes *like* one you have watched. View a David Attenborough wildlife special, and the EPG may offer you other natural history content. What does this do to traditional channels like the BBC, Channel 4 or RTE? Possibly they get taken out of the equation altogether. Why rely on a channel to aggregate quality content and deliver it to you, when you can do it

---

[62] I know some will argue that the Internet is older, and they'd be right: I'm only concerned with public as opposed to special interest use of the technology).

[63] Figures quoted in the Economist.

---

yourself (or programme the technology to do it). You might end up buying from a programme production company (imagine an Attenborough Wild Things Co) direct. We'll look at the distraction effects of this personalisation of content in more detail later. For the moment, it's enough to point out that there are serious challenges afoot to the economics of the TV business model. Advertising may decline, or at least change radically and channels change shape and role as they struggle to add value. Other players may enter (Microsoft? Nokia?). It is hard to believe that this will not affect the format of (increasingly digital) TV content. And of course viewing habits will change as people discover that they can fast forward, save, skip, rate and retrieve programmes and elements within them. Content creators will inevitably respond to this. PVRs are just one example of technology change continuing to affect media content. Others include wireless networking (especially at home), the rising adoption of broadband Internet access and significant changes to the capabilities of mobile devices. In fact the BBC are wo0rking on providing retrospective access to all their programmes for seven days over the Internet. As one of their managers recently said to me, "in the near future all TV will either be live or on demand". The schedule is dead.

The introduction of mobile into the ecology of the media world further complicates the picture. So the third reason why we can confidently expect further experimentation and disruption in media and content formats is that no medium works alone. We live in what is called a "cross platform" environment. In other words the Internet, TV, radio, film, DVD, music, mobile, even newspapers, are all interdependent. Change in one medium or platform will affect all the others sooner or later. All compete for our attention, yet feed off each other too. The BBC, previously best known as a broadcast organisation, now also runs the most popular news web site in Europe (www.bbc.co.uk/news). Reality TV depends on interaction via the phone for both the format to work and new revenue streams (money is made from the calls and texts). Mobile ringtones are sold from websites. The most significant commercial event in the world of digital communication has been Apple's development of a multi-platform vertical business model based on music. Through Apple a music lover can now:

- listen to music via software on their PC or Mac that can also record off a CD inserted in the computer (iTunes)
- buy music for download via Apple Musicstore (viewed only through iTunes)
- consume it on the go with an iPod
- manage their music (rate it with one to five stars, create playlists of multiple tracks)

Apple give you the software, hardware and the shop too. Each bit exists where it can work hardest for the customer. Cleverly Apple has avoided the web with its more restricted browser interfaces, and developed software (iTunes) fit for the job (and no other). Actually, Apple also furnish great examples of the thrust towards deep media which we'll see in a moment.

So despite the massive changes of the last ten years we can see that there is room for further disruptive change in digital media. The rush to commercialise in the late 90's, followed swiftly by the "dot com" collapse, killed off design experimentation as pretty much everyone sought first to get rich quick and then to get out quick. The recession of the early 2000's is now waning. The time feels right to push for greater depth to be designed into the new media which surround us. In what ways can this be done?

Introduce storytelling wherever possible

Stories illuminate our understanding by permitting the light of narrative to play on the world and the roles we perform in it. It has often been said that through stories mankind makes sense of what is around him, which is why storytelling has existed in all cultures in all recorded time. Many critics believe that there are a few essential plots: a recent book by Christopher Booker narrows the list down to " The Seven Basic Plots"[64] – Overcoming the Monster, Rags to Riches, The Quest, Voyage and Return, Comedy, Tragedy and Rebirth. This quote from Jung narrows the essence of stories down even further: "the treasure which the hero fetches from the dark cavern is life: it is himself".

Stories help us absorb ideas because we have learned to understand the structures that are used to construct them and can relate to a cast of characters. When a narrator sets the scene we know intuitively what he or she is doing. Likewise we expect an ending of some kind to a narration. In between we are sure characters will appear and interact. American literary critic Harold Bloom goes further. He thinks (controversially) that one writer in particular told stories so well that he effectively invented the way we see ourselves. The author in question is Shakespeare and in "Shakespeare – the Invention of the Human"[65] Bloom credits him with actually creating the way in which we see our personalities now, through his galaxy of characters parading across the stage, in and out of tragedy and comedy. Whether Bloom is right or wrong is not the point here: he is a very influential and admired literary critic who sincerely believes that life has imitated art in the most profound way it could. It is testimony to the power of stories.

Men and women throughout history have known the power of stories and symbolism and used it to their advantage: Canute, Danish king of England famously

---

[64] Continuum 2004
[65] Fourth Estate

took his court to the shoreline and in front of them ordered the tide to retreat. The sea refused to obey. Canute succeeded in his objective, which was to convey to his nobles that there were natural limits to what kings could achieve. It's such a good story we still learn it in school. Jesus used stories or parables to convey to his disciples his teachings. Aesop wrote fables in Ancient Greece to capture ideas. Every time an executive says "let's go for the low hanging fruit" he or she refers (probably unthinkingly) to the fable of the Fox and the Grapes. Which also persists as a popular pub name in England.

To date, the effect of digital has been to undermine or avoid the power of narrative. There are powerful reasons why. The first is that hypertext – the ability to create links to other documents or places has the effect of taking us away from where we are. It's hard to keep on the road of narrative, either as author or reader, when you know it is possible to follow alternative paths, and convenient junctions are offered. This was celebrated by the adoption of the metaphor "surfing" in the early days of the world wide web to describe the experience of moving with little effort from one place to another, following links to unexpected places as it were on a wave of surface level interest. "Browsing" conveys a similar and bovine approach to consumption.

This can be very empowering. A lot of the thinking in this book has been developed by following unanticipated directions of thought on the web. Try looking for information on pretty much any subject you care to choose and the web can shine numerous sidelights for you, intricately meshed together. The flip side is that very few people expect to read a web site in its entirety. Conscious that there are multiple escape routes close at hand, perhaps our brains are too hungry for new information and experiences to focus on what is in front of us, once we think we know what it is.

The second reason why narrative is at a discount in digital media is that, so far at least, those media have not been very immersive. Screen size is a factor. Cinemas retain audiences partly because the size of the screen, the dark, the volume of sound and the comfy chairs all combine to overwhelm us. People say "go and see it while it's still in the cinema – it's a big screen sort of film".[66] But it cannot just be screen size: years ago I saw South Park: The Movie on an airline seatback and howled with laughter – to the discomfort of a colleague next to me watching something else. The fact I did not notice his reaction demonstrates that I was certainly immersed in the film despite the size of the screen. Is it the hardware? But DVDs can play just as well on a PC as a DVD player. It may be the software: HTML simply does not allow for the creation of very immersive experiences, though Flash and other tools do permit greater use of movement and sound.

---

[66] The Lord of the Rings trilogy is a good example

Mark Curtis

The immersion problem is probably a combination of issues among which are:

- habit (we are accustomed to thinking of the PC as a research or work tool where we do tasks rather than enjoy ourselves)
- context (as a result of the above we use PC's in places where we do not expect narrative to be part of the environment, like at work)
- screen size and software limitations
- a history of restricted bandwidth limiting our expectations

So how could stories become part of the mix? Perhaps the project is impossible now that digital has given us the perfect tool for narrative deconstruction. I don't think so.

There are four ways I can think of.

The first – and I know this may sound a bit lame – is simply to make a renewed effort to use new technology to tell stories as its delivery capability improves in the near future. When TV advertising discovered story telling, 30 second sales messages became a lot more powerful – remember the Levis launderette? Mobile media may provide a natural place to do this as it is a very live and personal medium – imagine narrative that comes to you across the day or week. Viewers of a TV soap opera might subscribe to the diary of their favourite character, arriving daily on their phone as an MMS.

This leads on to the second source of narrative energy: time. The web is not a very compelling medium: things rarely happen "live" (with the exception of webcasts). Mobile devices change all that, encouraging the consumption of more time based events – which is why SMS alerts of things like football scores or news have proved so popular.

Time is important to people, and the third place where story telling is already reviving and taking on new shapes is from users themselves. There are signs that this is already happening – blogging is the prime example – most blogs are time based in their basic navigation. The Nokia product, Lifeblog[67], puts time at the heart of the experience.

Lastly – and there is a huge paradox here – story telling can be enabled by a greater use of context (more on this in a moment). The paradox is of course that adding in lots of context might have the effect of distracting us from central themes and direction. Nonetheless stories gain power from context or else most books could tell

---

[67] www.nokia.com/lifeblog

their tale in a few pages. War and Peace is long, and we bother to finish it, precisely because we enjoy the contextual fat around the narrative bones. It is time to flesh out digital content too.

Create beauty, apply humour, be playful

There is a hard edge to new communications technologies that needs softening. Thought of so often as an information carrier this is not surprising. Information is a currency we worship, and the high priests appear to have little time for aesthetics. It does not have to be so.

If the new communications technologies were only a tool for doing functional things (connecting, buying, calculating, downloading), then perhaps there would little room playfulness (though even that is questionable). But we are increasingly using these technologies for all sorts of creative expression, often personal, as we shall see. If we reverse the question, why should these new media not be a joy to look at and fun to experience? Such strongly worded notions normally NEVER appear in a design brief. Thus we find ourselves in a place where our expectations are modelled more around the design values of information media such as Yellow Pages. We should be aiming at least for a level of Vogue magazine, the Audi TT, the Bilbao Guggenheim, or Baz Luhrman's Romeo and Juliet. These should be the markers for digital inspiration. To repeat for the benefit of purists: this should never be at the expense of usability.

How? Largely it is ambition. Danny Brown won the prestigious Design Museum award for designer of the year in 2004 for his work on the web[68]. The work is experimental in a number of ways and definitely ambitious. More interesting work (by John Maeda) can be seen at www.maedastudio.com. It may take a while for such ideas to cross over to the mainstream that most people experience. Again I think this is down to evolution: new media just has not got there yet. Mail order clothing company Howies create a paper brochure. Each year this outstanding booklet is a pleasure to read and look at – packed with great pictures, insights and witty comments – oh and nice clothes too. Catalogues have been around for a long time so there is plenty of experience for designers to draw on. The attitude behind Howies ("the third biggest clothing company in Cardigan Bay") also drives creativity on paper at a level that is rare on web sites. It'll come.

The inspiration will also come from personal content. Some of the most interesting photography you can see is now on blogs. Outstanding examples can be found easily at www.photoblogs.org[69]. Most people I know add beauty to their lap-

---

[68] http://www.play-create.com
[69] For direct examples try www.hchamp.com and www.ephemera.org

Mark Curtis

tops by changing the "desktop" background to a photograph of their own (mine currently shows a two and a half metre wide paella cooking in a Spanish village square – my idea of beauty). Digital humour certainly exists – it is created and distributed by individuals, often in the form of viral messages. Sometimes these can be annoyingly unfunny – but no more so than a mate in the pub telling a poor joke. Large corporations have frequently tried to ban this kind of activity on their networks and equipment – I think we need more humour not less.[70]

It would be especially encouraging to see software get playful. Again – Apple experiment in a small way with this with icons that explode in a cloud when deleted. More please. A few years ago Salon Magazine decided to explore what it would be like if the on-screen messages our computers give us when things go wrong were replaced by Haiku – the three line Japanese poem which always express a profound and simple thought. Instead of "Error type 28: Invalid Action" or something similar, contributors suggested messages such as

"First snow, then silence.
This thousand dollar screen dies
So beautifully".
And
"A crash reduces
your expensive computer
to a simple stone".

We can be so po-faced about technology and end up having a miserable time with our screens, or we can mess about a bit. I know which I prefer.[71]

Reveal context

We have explored in an earlier chapter how context often goes awol on planet digital. I've also just suggested that it can add to narrative. Like stories and beauty, we need to make a conscious effort to design context back into the media. Information is abundant, but much more valuable, and meaningful, in context. We've seen the tendency to present information, with little concern for provenance.

Is this Beethoven?

011000000101010101011111010101010101010101010101010101010101010101010101010
10101010101101111111000000010101010101010101000011110000110101010110100

---

[70] Of course there is plenty out there if you know where to look. Find it at www.snackspot.com, www.angryalien.com
[71] But then I'm not the IT director of a large corporation

Or this?

How to add context? The most powerful conceptual weapon is a question – how can we make the invisible visible? This can happen in all sorts of ways. A good example is above: why not provide visuals to go along with the music files that people now keep on their computers. Encouragingly, Apple has thought of this, and iTunes has a space for "song artwork". At http://www.sprote.com/clutter you can download some very cool free software which allows Apple users to pile up CD covers on their desktop for instant access – double clicking on the cover starts the music from within iTunes. You can also use this to find favourites visually – a method I referred to earlier in the chapter on context. Expect more of this, because people want context to their music and record companies desperately need to add value to compete with free file sharing. Not just pictures but other, currently invisible, stuff. This might include peer ratings of songs and recommendations derived from these. If Radiohead fans typically also listen to The Pixies then that could be useful information to anyone who falls into either category. If you don't mind Apple knowing what you listen to in return for such a service, then it becomes both possible and valuable.

An interesting attempt to give exactly this kind of data some tangibility is Audioscrobbler.[72] It describes itself thus: "Audioscrobbler is a computer system that builds up a detailed profile of your musical taste. After installing an Audioscrobbler Plugin, your computer sends the name of every song you play to the Audioscrobbler

---

[72] http://www.audioscrobbler.com/about.php

Server. With this information, the Audioscrobbler server builds you a 'Musical Profile'. Statistics from your Musical Profile are shown on your Audioscrobbler User Page, available for everyone to view. There are lots of people using Audioscrobbler, but usually only the people who like the same sort of music to you are interesting. The Audioscrobbler Server calculates which people are most similar to you, based on shared musical taste, so you can take a look at what your peers are listening to. With this information, Audioscrobbler is able to automatically generate suggestions for new songs/artists you might like. These suggestions are based on the same principals as Amazon's "People who bought this also bought X,Y,Z", but because the Audioscrobbler data is what people are actually listening to, the suggestions tend to make more sense than Amazon."

Using a system called Musicompass,[73] this data is then visualised as interactive maps of musical taste. A similar service can be found at Musicplasma[74] As services these probably won't change the world, but two very interesting trends emerge. One is that Audioscrobbler uses the power of social networks to build helpful context. The use made of technology by social networks, as I will argue later, is a reason to feel very optimistic. The other pointer is that both services have discovered a way to make previously hidden data useful and attractive. This data may even create links between people which did not exist before, thus helping to build new kinds of social network.

Devices that know their context is another area where we can expect to see many developments. Mobile phones provide extraordinary data, most of which remains invisible. What could be done with it? In the future you will be able to look at a map of where you went, every day of your life, of what media you consumed and when. Graphic representations of who you call and text could help give you a contextual picture of your relationships, allowing you to review and reconsider what you do, who you interact with. Imagine being able to point your cameraphone – or any device with a lens connected to the network for that matter – at anything, and doing a search on it. It's being worked on at the University of Southern California's Information Sciences Institute.[75] The nickname is Visual Google. The technical barriers are obviously pretty high, but it seems to me that this once again changes our feelings about space around us. It's a subtly different vision from the idea that everything is connected. In this scenario, everything can have its context explored or added to on the fly…

In fact being able to *see* context may also become a key part of exploring your relationship with other people and their content. In this way deep media can be a

---

[73] http://www.musicompass.net
[74] http://www.musicplasma.com
[75] The Feature.com January 13th 2005

way of developing trust. Brown and Duguid[76] have commented on the difficulties experienced developing digital trust. Their focus is on material documents which "not only serve to make information but also to warrant it – to give it validity…for information has trouble testifying on its own behalf. Its only recourse in the face of doubt is to add more information. Yet people do not add much to their credibility by insisting "I'm telling the truth". Nor does it help much to write "good" on the face of a check. Piling up information from the same source doesn't always increase reliability…In general, people look beyond information to triangulate reliability. People look past what others say, for example, to gauge trustworthiness. Some clues might be formal and institutional: who does a prospective client work for? What is her credit rating? Others are informal, such as dress, address and cars…In a similar way people look beyond the information in documents."

To where? To the weight of the document,[77] its print quality, any marks and traces of age. All these are context, and most are usually hard or impossible to see in the digital world. This does not need to be the case: if we recognise the need for context we may be able to design it in. The data is usually there. Could "files" come with covers? Could these give a sense of their size more tangible than a number of kilobytes? Might some documents fade over time to indicate age? How about a system for seeing who else has read or added to a document recently, or where it has been? Where did it originate from? How many times has it been copied?[78] Of course not all of these will be useful all the time. But they add depth to our understanding of, and relationship with, digital content.

Design "body language" into the experience

As most people know, body language conveys a rich range of emotions. We all understand each other better when we can decipher non-verbal communication. A touch of the nose – famously – usually means deception. A raised eyebrow indicates scepticism or surprise. Leaning forward often signals engagement. In fact we have developed a range of sophisticated muscle movements to supplement the words we use. Much of this disappears in electronically mediated communication.

Academic analysis of the events leading to the disastrous decision to launch the Challenger mission in 1986 (the rocket exploded shortly after take-off) has shown quite how much misunderstanding and misinterpretation can happen when body

---

[76] The Social Life of Information

[77] There is something about the physical presence of a big book, or a tapestry for instance, that tells us humans were involved in its production, and that they cared enough to make the effort. Can the same be said for most web sites? Ephemerality suggests less importance.

[78] Much of this data is already standard in say, a Microsoft Word document if you know where to look. But we've not yet found ways to make it explicit and useful…

Mark Curtis

language is not visible. The decision depended on telephone conferences between the Flight Centers in Alabama and Florida and engineers in Utah. Distance and vocal pressure meant that the "engineers missed the signs of Mulloy's and Hardy's (the decision makers) uncertainty and willingness to listen". These signs were, according to those present, visually unmistakable. As a result, the engineers withdrew opposition to the launch, which went ahead.[79]

The lesson from this is that we should design communications technologies which allow us to *communicate* better. Half of good communication is listening – this is often forgotten. In the Challenger example, accurate listening was hard because the participants only had words and tone to go on, and could not triangulate meaning against other physical clues. Yet in small ways software can demonstrate listening of a kind: increasingly a standard of good design is that icons respond to the user when a cursor is rolled over them to demonstrate that they are active, or a suitable target for dropping another item. In a sense the computer is saying: "yes I know you are there and I'm giving you hints on what you can do". Another tiny example is the tick on older Nokia phones which tells you that a task such as saving a telephone number has been completed. It's the digital equivalent of a nod.[80]

Digital body language can be even more explicit. Many people will be familiar with the problem of e-mail causing unintended offence. The brevity of the medium and the ease with which it is used sometimes cause real problems because recipients fail to distinguish the intended meaning clearly. Sarcasm or heavy handedness is often diagnosed when the writer simply was in a rush. Early users of e-mail understood this: and the result were emoticons such as ☺ ☻ ☹. I have not tracked the early history of these, but guess that they evolved from someone experimenting with keyboard combinations in order to express happiness, gloom, irony (my favourite – the raised eyebrow). It is interesting to note that hundreds of years of letter writing in the west had not developed emoticons. They came with digital. Apart from truncated words in text messaging it is hard to think of any other innovations such as this.[81]

---

[79] Original research by Diane Vaughan, this example is drawn from the excellent "In Good Company" (HBS Press) by Don Cohen and Laurence Prusak which argues for a greater attention to the invisible social capital that makes organisations work well.

[80] A related issue is to note how, when a consumer tries to deal with a company on-line, they so rarely acknowledge the precise problem. You might receive a response saying: "thank you for your contact. Our customer services team are dealing with your issue and will contact you in no more than 36 hours." However people gifted in communication often repeat back to an interlocutor a summary of their issue)"I think you are saying that…", so why not use this simple technique in e-mail? This might take the form of "We got your mail. You say your issue is that the book never arrived. OK – we are onto this and will get back to you by tomorrow at the latest. Thanks".

[80] Matt Webb (www.interconnected.org) is experimenting with what he has dubbed "glancing", a rapid way of acknowledging other people who you know and are on-line at the same time.

Yet they are surely there to be had: how for instance could we use colour to express more meaning through electronic communication? What other uses could we make of icons beyond the ubiquitous smileys? Instant messenger software is beginning to explore this. If video phones take off, what could we communicate with the keypad even while we hold the device and talk into the camera? Warmth? Frustration? Agreement? Enthusiasm? Love? If this sounds strange, consider that it may only be because we take a utilitarian view of the technology, and have still to explore its full communications potential. Even if it is quixotic to expect digital to replace or reproduce body language, an achievable ambition would be to augment conversations in new and deep ways.

Respect design conventions that make it easy for people

It is very distracting to have to learn new ways to do achieve a goal. Over time, web designers discovered that navigational links were best placed at the top and left hand side of web pages. This may have been based on natural readability issues, or a gradual consensus – probably it was both. This has become a convention. It is unusual to see the main areas of a web site listed for the user on the right hand side of a page. One expects to see a logo of some kind at the top left hand side of a site. Elsewhere, when clicked, this should lead back to the home page. This doesn't mean that not doing any of these is wrong: simply that if a designer chooses to challenge convention he or she should have good reason to do so.

Right across digital a lot has been learnt and as a result some basic rules have emerged. User expectations need to be respected. A triangle on its side pointing to the right on audio or video software and hardware means "press/click here to play". Two thick vertical bars mean "pause". It makes sense to use these everywhere appropriate as it costs users a lot less time to learn their way around. Perhaps this sounds too obvious (it will to designers). If so, why are new devices and services often hard to get to grips with? Partly it is because conventions have not been used or respected.

Mobile is very prone to this – and the problem is likely to get worse before it gets better. Coming to, or even already on a phone near you, is a range of applications and functions which will seriously complicate life – if you use them. These might include new games, video messaging, video calling, location messaging, music downloading and playback, a wallet containing digital cash, perhaps your keys too. Let's imagine you have a Nokia (in Europe up to 40% of people do) running what the company calls Series 60, which is the platform for the larger screen colour phones such as the 7210 and 6630. If you have been using it for a while your thumb will have become accustomed to the basic key combinations: that the two top keys (generally) are for choices and action, that generally the menu choices are "options" and "select" for the left key, and "back", "cancel" or "exit" for the right key. This

Mark Curtis

is pretty consistent right across the applications that Nokia put on the phones such as the camera, profiles, call log, contacts. Once however other parties bring their applications to the phone none of this is guaranteed. There is a fascinating war of sorts taking place between the major handset manufacturers (especially Nokia) and operators over who should control the phone interface. Microsoft is a combatant too as they wish their system to be the winner – from a design perspective one hopes they don't win. Re-learning the basic rules of interaction for everything you do on your mobile device will only add to distraction.

A deep media approach will be hampered by inconsistent conventions: that is why it is a rule to respect users.

Simplify all the time

My colleague Olof Schybergson brings this rule to life. What, he asks, is a kitchen for? Not to be a kitchen, but for cooking and eating in. Consider poor kitchens, often great for showing off the owner's expensive taste but utterly useless for the business end of things. Now imagine that the core things you need to do in a kitchen (perhaps prepare, heat, serve) were obfuscated or hidden by twenty five other potential activities and their signage (freeze!, grind!, store!, soak! mix! Etc..). Bad design frequently does this in the digital world.

Good tests for simplicity are:
- is it clear what this product does?
- can I do things quickly?

Apple has been brilliant in this respect. The iPod has just five "buttons" and the dial. As of today, I Tunes is in its fourth iteration, and has had small but significant additions at each software release. From the start it was clear that it played music on your computer. Later a shop was added, and most recently quick links to information on each artist. The effect has been to add complexity, but at an easy to absorb pace. Layered complexity means that advanced options are there for power users if they really want it, but novices are not confronted with it.

Deep media then is an approach to communications technology which seeks to humanise our electronic interaction as far as is possible and desirable. There will always be constraints. However as long as mankind seeks meaning then stories, beauty, context and a sense of body language are worth striving for. So long of course as these don't obfuscate the point. Is there not then a risk that deep media actually increase distraction – taking us further away from the real? Perhaps, but the intent is to replace the superficial with meaning, allowing us better choice over what to engage with and more fulfilment from what we do.

PART TWO
The Social Potential Of New Technology

Chapter Nine
Deep Media

Deep Media is about enhancing content. This chapter is about enhancing our sense of self. The post modern world teaches us to believe that there is no one truth or reality. We'll look at how equally a single sense of self is becoming harder to cling to, and as with so many other contemporary trends, digital communications mirror and encourage this. On the Internet, we can be lots of people and switch, mix, pretend and even steal identity easily. Kids do this especially; for instance at the very popular Habbo Hotel. The Internet allows us to distribute our sense of self too via web cams and now blogs. It seems that there is an interesting reversal going on: things we did publicly become private, private matters become public. As a consequence privacy becomes less important, and this too has an impact on our sense of who we are. We'll see that may be that we are happy to trade privacy for security, which, optimistically, is less threatening than it sounds.

Who am I?

Do modern media distract us from a sense of who we "truly" are? Already in 1950 Pope Pius X11 thought so. Quoted by Marshall McLuhan he said "It is not an exaggeration to say that the future of modern society and the stability of its inner life depend in large part on the maintenance of an equilibrium between the strength of the techniques of communication and the capacity of an individual's own reaction."

In his influential book "The Saturated Self"[82] published in 1991, US academic Kenneth J. Gergen investigates what he calls "dilemmas of identity in modern life". Although he writes just before the rise of the Internet, Gergen already anticipates much of its effect. He points to two core trends – social immersion and media saturation.

---

[82] Basic Books

Social Immersion

It is almost a cliché now to compare social life with 200 years ago, so I won't dwell on the massive difference between a largely peasant world whose mental and community boundaries were mainly set by geography, and now. But comparisons reveals how fast we are moving. The sheer number of people one can potentially interact with has exploded. Consider the increasing opportunities for interaction given by:

Railways
Public postal services
The car
The telephone
Radio broadcasting
Films
Printed books
Airplanes
Television

Gergen lists these as the 19th and 20th century technologies of "social saturation". "Each brought people into increasingly close proximity, exposed them to an increasing range of others, and fostered a range of relationships that could never have occurred before".
Now consider more recent developments and their impact.

- Increased long distance travel occasions (dramatically lower airfares in real terms)
- The massive increase in participation in further education (at least in the UK)
- e-mail
- Mobile phones (calls and text)
- Web sites (especially blogs, forums)
- Instant messaging

All of these mean simply that we *meet* a larger number of people than our ancestors, and have the opportunity to communicate with many more. As well as the complexity of trying to deal with these acquaintances, their names, faces, habits, personal history and contact details, often different technologies are used and we have to invest effort to master them and their etiquette too. The latter takes time to evolve and in some cases the correct behaviour is still emergent. How do you sign off an e-mail? Is "yours sincerely" still appropriate or now too formal? Many of the Nordic people I work with finish an e-mail with the enigmatic "br". It took a while to understand that this was not a statement of how cold it was up north, but shorthand for "best regards". I've adopted the latter (longhand) as it seems to be acceptable and fit the medium. Teens famously use abbreviations in txt msgs 2 save precious characters (a text can only contain160). Is it OK for a man in his forties to use such shorthand, or does it look like mutton posing as lamb?

These are real social issues grabbing our attention. Each one looks insignificant on its own: once again it is the accumulation of them that is important. How quickly does one respond to personal communication? Answers vary, but it is clear that expectations have risen, driven by the immediacy of digital media. I've had people complain because I did not answer an e-mail within 24 hours. Friends in large companies report similar implicit pressure. At the very least one might expect a text message to elicit a response (if one is required) within two to three hours.

So we find ourselves communicating in more ways with more people more often. Each effort requires subtle or sometimes quite major shifts in register (the voice and language we choose to use). Given the amazing potential of our brains to absorb information and communicate, we should be able to deal with this. Except for the fact that there are only 24 hours in a day, as busy people often seem to say.

Media Saturation

Layered on top of social immersion are the sheer number of mediated images and messages thrown at us, and that we choose to engage with. You'd have to be a hermit not to notice the proliferation of media in modern life. Hundreds of digital TV channels, new radio stations enabled by the Internet and DAB,[83] millions of web sites, video screens in buses, on airplanes, mobile spam: most of these did not exist 15 years ago. Our sense of self is surely challenged by the relentless bombardment of ideas, sounds and images. Much of it is very attractive – perhaps more so than the reality of our daily lives. It has probably always been so, since media were invented. Who can doubt that small boys have always thrilled to the exploits of their heroes, be they Nelson (through newspapers and songs) or Shane (film, books), or Beckham (live, TV, video) and imagined themselves in some immersive way to be that person? Surely such perfectly natural imaginings change their sense of potential, of self in subtle ways. Billy Liar is just one of many fictional characters to have investigated his sense of self through fantasy.

In "Books Do Furnish A Room"[84] novelist Anthony Powell explores man's addiction to role playing. Writing of one character, the author X Trapnel, he tell us

---

[83] Digital Audio Broadcasting
[84] Arrow

---

that he "wanted, among other things, to be a writer, a dandy, a virtuoso, a good chap, a man of honour, a hard case, a spendthrift, an opportunist, a *raisonneur*; to be very rich, to be very poor, to possess a thousand mistresses, to win the heart of one love to whom he was ever faithful, to be on the best of terms with all men, to avenge savagely the lightest affront, to live to a hundred full years and honour, to die young and unknown but recognized the next day as the most neglected genius of the age." Later, exploring the "essence" of Trapnel, Powell takes the idea further. "...he managed to retain in a reasonably flourishing state-flourishing that is, in his own eyes,-what General Conyers would have called his 'personal myth', that imaginary state of being already touched on in Trapnel's case. The General, speaking one felt with authority, always insisted that, if you bring off adequate preservation of your personal myth, nothing much else in life really matters. It is not what happens to people that is significant, but what they think happens to them."

With his characteristic elegance and tautness of language, Powell captures a truth of the human condition. Identity is not static, but malleable and composed of – sometimes many – concepts that can even pull us in opposite directions. Where do these stereotypes come from? Largely they come not from direct observation of the world about us, but instead through media. I've never met a real fighter pilot, but always wanted to be one after seeing the film "Battle of Britain" when I was eight. Gergen again: "It is undoubtedly true that for many people film relationships provide the most emotionally wrenching experiences of the average week. The ultimate question is not whether media relationships approximate the normal in their significance, but whether normal relationships can match the powers of artifice."

We are more immersed in media than ever before, offered a greater number of potential selves to consider for adoption, adaptation or rejection. As Gergen points out "emerging technologies saturate us with the voices of humankind – both harmonious and alien. As we absorb their varied rhymes and reasons, they become part of us and we of them. Social saturation furnishes us with a multiplicity of incoherent and unrelated languages of the self. For everything we "know to be true" about ourselves, other voices within respond with doubt and even derision. This fragmentation of self conceptions corresponds to a multiplicity of incoherent and disconnected relationships. These relationships pull us in myriad directions, inviting us to play such a variety of roles that that the very concept of an "authentic self" with knowable characteristics recedes from view. The fully saturated self becomes no self at all".

To compound these effects, social immersion and media saturation are moving together as trends. As we participate more in media, helping interactively to shape its content, then social contact and media become if not the same, then very tightly intertwined. For example when I read and leave a comment on someone else's blog (an interactive web journal), is that an act of social immersion or media saturation?

Mark Curtis

When a journalist invites feedback by printing their e-mail address at the end of an article, they are part of a process that is driving us closer to the media, and the media to our social networks.

Sense of self can and does change

Sense of self is important because it profoundly affects the way we view the world, which in turn brings bias to our actions and determines the choices we make. It is important to establish that identities are concepts constructed by society to meet its needs, not fixed and immutable laws of life. If we look at other cultures or even previous periods of our own, we can find an enormous variation of what people accept as "obviously true" about themselves. For instance some historians believe that romantic love (in Western culture) was more or less invented by the courtly circles of medieval Languedoc, and given voice by the troubadour tradition. Different, perhaps more pragmatic notions of intimate relationships, suited to prevailing conditions, had held sway until then in Europe. This may be why west and east so frequently fail to understand each other. Ideas that are norms in other cultures (for instance the importance of "face" in China, the seeming acceptance of death in India) are hard for us to grasp precisely because we have no real equivalent. Naming of children differs radically from culture to culture: in Bali names are principally used to signal membership of kinship groups and social status (e.g.: first born). This must surely affect how individuals perceive their identity, and relationships to others. Gergen also lists words and phrases that are used routinely to frame identity in the modern world – low self esteem, repressed, seasonal affective disorder, post traumatic stress disorder, bulimic, mid life crisis. As he points out, none of these were in common use before the last century, and they all belong to a vocabulary of mental problems, which has been growing. It seems that our sense of self can and does change, and as we invent the words to describe the new conditions, so the words fix the ideas in our minds.

Gergen argues that until quite recently two basic types of identity held sway. The romantic identity has its roots in the nineteenth century. Typical vocabulary associated with this kind of self is 'passion', 'soul' and 'creative'. The modernist self, as the name implies, is a twentieth century creation with roots in the enlightenment. Words that the modernist self would use include 'rational', 'reason' and 'opinions'. However a new intellectual tradition, on the rise for last forty to fifty years is challenging romantic and modernist identities. It is post-modernism.[85] In the post modern world, nothing is "true", statements are merely viewpoints, angles, perspectives: in short ideas are "constructs" built out of words. "The post-modern condition…is

---

[85] Academic experts will have to forgive me here if I do not grasp all the subtle nuances of post modernism. Anyway, if I've understood it correctly, my interpretation is as true as theirs.

marked by a plurality of voices vying for the right to reality – to be accepted as legitimate expressions of the true and the good…It is a world where anything goes that can be negotiated." If this is the case for the news, art, literature, then is it also the case for us? If so, then the very notion of a fixed centre to one's identity is under threat. We become shifting sands. Once again it can be heard in the words we choose to employ. In feudal society very precise terms explained who you were: villein, serf, cottar, yeoman, knight, all of these connoted rights and responsibilities, social place. Industrial times eliminated most of these as redundant, and popularised new notions such as worker, manager, middle class, gentleman. These terms are also now on the wane. It is not clear what is replacing them. Such precise categorisation is harder to hang on to in post modern times. Even big defining categories such as "man" and "woman" are up for grabs in some academic and feminist quarters.

The rise of transsexuals seems to me to be a perfect example of how what is "obviously true" can change. One hundred years ago it would have been barely thinkable that changing sex might one day be possible. Few, if any, people would have believed that although you may externally be a man, inside you could be a "woman trapped in a man's body" as the contemporary cliché has it.

Digital identity distraction

If what is true can only be understood by accepting simultaneously that there are compelling (and true) alternatives, then the new digital media can add hugely to levels of distraction, because they make so many more alternative views available to us. This cuts both ways: communications technology has played a key role in undermining our belief in objective truth, and the uses we put the new communications technologies to reveal our post modern instincts to deny that there is one single sustainable truth.

Media have made it harder to hang on to single points of view in two ways – by expanding what we can engage with mentally, and by vastly increasing what we can hear. In the first case, travel and mass media allow us to expand our thinking beyond parochial concerns and limited horizons. And when we do, we can hear more voices "daring to question the old and institutionalised truths". If this sounds like "travel broadens the mind" then it is (if we define media consumption as a form of travel). The famous Baghdad blog of the recent Iraq war is a classic example of how we can also hear tongues from near and far challenge the messages that those in power may have defined.

What of the usage we make of these new technologies? How do these reveal the new mindset? The Internet provides amazing opportunities to experiment with identity, many of which have been well documented since before usage broke into the mainstream. It is well known that some men take the opportunity to pretend to be women on-line (and vice versa), often for nefarious reasons, but also sometimes to explore a feminine side to their personality that for whatever reason they feel uncomfortable revealing in "real" life. The activities of paedophiles, "grooming" young people by pretending to be their peers, has also been well covered. At a less sinister level many ordinary users prefer pretend names on-line. A quick look at two on-line discussion groups revealed

Baabaa5

Spacepig1

Flyrabbit

The Naked Genius

I bet they wish they didn't sell beckham

Blue since 42

El bandit

alongside some perfectly ordinary and probably real names.

On reflection, this is pretty harmless stuff, akin to giving oneself nicknames. Most people would probably not accept the idea that they are thereby adopting multiple identities on-line, but a significant few are doing so. The potential is there and it may be that younger people, growing up with it as a given, are the ones to watch.

Habbo Hotel is a very successful virtual world created for kids and teenagers. At last count it had one million active users in the UK, and outlets elsewhere too, notably Finland where it began. Participants can walk around, develop their own rooms, buy furnishings, set up businesses – in short mimic a lot of life in the physical world. They can buy and use credits to purchase items, and of course converse with each other. Almost all users have invented names. A very real problem for the managers of Habbo Hotel has been that some of their members twigged after a while that it was possible to steal other members' identity. They did this by a variety of means which included mailing the victim posing as the administrator or someone else, claiming that they knew of a way to increase their credits. All the hapless recipient had to do was to reveal their password. Which of course, some stupidly did, handing over their identity and therefore all their Habbo goods. Habbo identity scams can even be found on Google, which ironically is handy for the administrators who can act to block them off or alert users.

According to an ex-manager of Habbo, a lot of kids start off with four or more identities but give up after about three weeks, unable to continue to manage each persona fully or consistently. At this stage they refine to just one. So if Habbo is anything to go by, sense of self survives reasonably intact, if anything because it's just too exhausting to be multiphrenic. Regular users of networked technology will empathise with this. Managing the user names and passwords required to do anything with phone companies, banks, commercial web sites and discussion communities is a bit of a nightmare. Organisations demand different standards so it becomes very difficult only ever to use one name and password. For instance Mark Curtis is usually a name that has been taken on larger commercial web sites. Often they will offer a not very close substitute like MarkCurtis124, which is fine but I have to note it down somewhere, safe, because with all the others I have I'll never remember it. Then passwords always seem to differ in the number of characters required, whether numbers have to be mixed with letters or not, and case sensitivity. These too have to be recorded in a secure place. Have I become multiple people? Of course not, but my digital identity is quite hard to manage and takes up a fair amount of time – so the effect is still distracting.

Another aspect of Habbo is interesting. Friends use the Hotel as a meeting place to discuss things. Apparently when you ask a user if they know who they are talking to, interacting with, a typical response will be "Of course, I don't know any strangers". Have you met this person then? "No – a friend introduced me". The implication is that personal (and on-line) recommendation is good enough to form a relationship. Have the values of children changed, the boundaries been pushed back? I suspect not – children are probably neither more nor less receptive to form-ing new interesting relationships than 50 years ago. Much behaviour on Habbo is recognisable and predictable: girls tend to set up businesses, boys form gangs to take over rooms. 12 year olds aspire to be close to16 year olds, who take advantage by employing them as accolytes to work in virtual hairdressers. The real difference that Habbo symbolises is that knowing someone is so much easier, the opportunities to socialise infinitely extended around the world, 24 hours a day. Digital technology removes the physical constraint on how many relationships one can form. The aver-age amount of time users spend on Habbo in a session is 40 minutes. 40% spend two hours or more at a time. From this adult's point of view, that is an unthinkable amount of time to spend on a web site, but apparently users do not see it as just a web site. The spatial environment is critical to this illusion. For instance one can see users speaking in other rooms, but not overhear what they are saying. This is social immersion, digital style.

In summary then, digital media reinforce a contemporary trend away from a single, always true, sense of self.[86] It does this by offering many many more images and ideas of what one could be than ever before, and allowing users easily to experi-ment with alternative identities online. We should be cautious about over-emphasis-ing this latter point; it is not yet clear that we have enough time or mental energy to do it effectively. In a conference presentation titled "Social Software for Kids", Fiona Romeo points out that several studies conclude that after experimenting with

---

[86] It should be emphasised that it is not just new media which do this: our sense of self is also under siege from other trends, for instance the loss of jobs for a lifetime, the related growth of freelance/contract lifestyles, and the blurring of work with leisure. Science and medicine too head in this direction: if genetic engineering will allow us to programme out imperfection, or select for traits considered desir-able, what room then for glorious difference – the big nose? the glossy redhead? It would be sad indeed if the future holds homogeneity.

Mark Curtis

chatting to strangers, teenagers move back to instant messaging (where you talk to known contacts or friends of friends). Nonetheless these buddy lists can be up to 200 people long.[87] Managing identity and contacts in the digital era is time-consuming, and adds to the growing list of "things to do in order to do things."

Trust at risk?

Habbo is a microcosm of teenage life. Good and bad things happen there. More unusual is that your identity can be invented, changed or even stolen by someone else posing as somebody else. Are you who you say you are? Some of the uses made of digital media are destructive of trust, which in my view is unambiguously bad news, because trust is a key component of social capital.

Distance is part of the problem. Although, as we have seen already, writers have lauded the "death of distance", they may be penning its obituary notice too hastily. Distance diminishes responsibility. Humourist PJ O'Rourke once darkly observed that if you hit someone in a big car at least it all happens a long way away, like famine in the third world. How strong are social connections made without first hand knowledge of your correspondent? The medium has enormous reach, but little by way of reciprocity. In plain terms, some idiot in Florida can fill my e-mail inbox with spam and there is little I can do about it. A friend of mine once wrote to the Chairman of a company which routinely sent him junk mail. He had tried with no apparent success to remove himself from their mailing lists. This time he threatened to go round and personally dump all his unwanted mail on floor of the Chairman's office. The junk stopped immediately. I am not sure if there is an effective Internet equivalent, though people have tried to spam the spammers. How can one trust the company that chooses to use a computer to automatically phone and try to sell you something at home? How emotionally distant is that? Disney recently did this to a friend of mine, twice in a fortnight, and much to his annoyance. I bet if Michael Eisner was directly accessible by all the people his company's servers dial up, its behaviour would change.

Trust is diminished in other insidious ways. Context stripping is one: information flows around the net which has been cut and pasted from multiple sources. News no longer comes just from "trusted sources". When news items break, one can frequently get the story that news outlets won't tell by e-mail, or on unofficial web sites. But can you trust it, shorn of context? As we saw earlier, scams arrive frequently by e-mail or on your mobile phone. I'm quite sure that it would have been a noteworthy event for someone to attempt to con you 20 years ago. No longer is that the case.

---

[87] Presentation originally given to ETech 2004. http://foe.typepad.com/blog/children_and_teens/index.html

Trading Privacy

Questions of trust and identity lead inexorably to considerations of privacy in the digital age. Big changes in our notions of privacy may be underway. Susan Greenfield certainly believes so in her book "Tomorrow's People".[88] She imagines a future where we have explicitly traded privacy for information and security. There are some very clear pointers to this. Fear – especially of terrorism is a major feature of the early 21st century. We are not as safe as we thought in our skyscrapers or underground stations. The subject of the prestigious BBC Reith Lectures for 2004 was fear. Technology offers no escape from fear, but at least the promise of lessening risk. The UK government is noisily testing the idea of identity card schemes. Eye scans and digital recognition software are expected to become features of international travel.

Beyond an institutional response to the changing geo-political landscape, privacy has been softly undermined by the Internet. Again we are talking about *potential* here: the newfound ability to do things eventually breaks surface as a change in behaviour. Once you digitise information, it becomes easy to send, copy and read. Technical standards such as TCP/IP, web browsers, HTML, Windows, e-mail and GSM facilitate this because everybody is able to be part of the network and share. Once this happens, and everything is connected, the barriers to exchanging information are lowered. It is simply easier to share files and we all know it. What then do we seek to keep private? Many companies now maintain Intranets (web based internal information networks), Extranets (web sites with restricted access for selected outsiders) and public web sites. Much information is common to all three. If it can be published internally, it can easily become public too. The membrane is permeable, and the data flows.

A trend in large organisations is to use technology to push towards "real time" reporting so that managers can understand what is happening as close as possible to the moment when it happens. As this becomes a reality so shareholders (aware of the potential) may begin to demand it too. Ludicrous? Remember that standard reporting intervals of major publicly quoted companies have shifted in the last ten years from annual to quarterly, and that the Internet has seen the rise of the day trader, individuals who react hourly to business information to buy and sell shares profitably.

Individuals have also used the Internet to challenge the boundaries of privacy, usually their own. The web is a gift to the self-publicist and nobody saw that more clearly than the eponymous star of the Jennicam, now sadly closed. The Jennicam captured stills of an ordinary American girl's life as seen in her bedroom from

---

[88] Penguin Allen Lane

Mark Curtis

minute to minute, hour to hour, day to day. The pictures grabbed by her web cam were available 24/7 on a web site[89] so that millions worldwide could share in her existence – warts and all. The Jennicam was a precursor to the new generation of Blogs. A Blog is basically a web diary (weB LOG) of someone's life. Like a traditional journal it contains text and pictures. There are some important differences. Blogs are available (unless password protected) for all to see, authors can publish instantly (text and photos), they can offer links to other blogs or web sites, and often readers are encouraged to add their own annotations. What would the most famous diarist of all time, Samuel Pepys have made of all this? As he frequently wrote in a made up language, one can assume that he did not intend his private thoughts to be seen. Bloggers do. Blogging is growing fast – at the time of writing there were maybe 2 million individual blogs globally according to the Observer. Given that most people I meet have still not heard of them, there's no shortage of potential.

The Public/Private Inversion

What is going on may well be a massive inversion of public/private media and content. Things that we traditionally do privately seem to be going public, and those things that we do publicly are becoming matters of private contemplation. Conversations, once held in small spaces with limited numbers of people (even the pub fits this description) are now there for all to see on web forums, on-line communities of all shapes and sizes, messaging groups, reality TV shows, celebrity text messages (though they may not always wish their communications to be seen so widely), leaked government e-mails. Journals and personal memories are "published" to the web, in their millions.[90] New businesses are now being built around this.

Meanwhile personalised media increasingly bring us "public" content for consumption in our own space, and at a time of our choosing. Examples include shopping on the Internet (now showing real commercial signs of success after the initial hype and slump) the iPod (10,000 songs in your pocket), personal video recorders such as TiVO, text news alerts to your phone, simple phone conversations held in a public space. These are just the start, especially where hand held devices are concerned.

Plenty of observers believe that a result of this will be that the identity of the individual will increasingly be subsumed beneath that of the gigantic network of information and content – that we will become nodes in a system, recognisable only

---

[89] The archives are still there: www.jennicam.org

[90] The highest profile recent event, a classic of its type was Alistair Campbell's mistake in February 2005, accidentally sending BBC journalists an e-mail from his Blackberry handheld which read "Fuck off and cover something important you twats!"

for the role we play in the greater whole, the content we provide. I'm not sure about taking this thought to such extremes (though understanding networks has become very important and we'll come on to that later.) What are Blogs if not humans affirming their identity to the widest audience they can? Nevertheless the vision suggests that we will increasingly live our lives *within* information technology and this feels more likely. As suggested earlier in this book, our changing ideas of space are preparing the ground for such a change.

Being Watched

This is not necessarily as worrying as it initially sounds. Privacy and conspiracy nuts get very heated about ideas like identity cards, but it's hard to see what the problem is if you have nothing to hide. In many areas technology will permit some very desirable observation. Aware (through intense media coverage) of the fears parents have for their children in public spaces, one of my daughters "invented" a mobile monitoring system for kids when she was 12. She assumed that mobile phones know where you are at all times. In effect they do, though it's the operator who has the information – to about 300 metre accuracy in town and improving. She reasoned that parents would pay good money to know where their teenage offspring are at any given moment, and that teenagers may trade this for the benefit of a phone. She's not the only one to have figured this out, and private and public institutions worldwide are looking at it as a system to deter all kinds of crime. In Denmark amusement park Tivoli Gardens uses just such a technology to reassure parents that they cannot lose their children. Its Child Spotter Service is now renting out Bluetooth enabled (Bluetooth is a wireless connecting protocol) wristband tags to parents for their children. The parents simply register their mobile phone number. If a child goes awol, the parents send an SMS asking after the particular tag, and get an text back telling them where their little darling has wandered off to. Legoland is running a similar scheme using WiFi.

This is an interesting model for how privacy might be invaded: not necessarily by the state, sometimes by corporations (with permission) and (as per my daughter's example) mainly by individual people, co-operating together. Wouldn't the local anti burglar scheme Neighbourhood Watch be more powerful if monitoring and reporting was enabled by digital technology?

Old people – not known generally for their rapid adoption of technology – might also be beneficiaries. Exploring this issue with my colleagues we developed an idea that brings it to life. Nothing in this is fanciful.

Mark Curtis

Guardian Angels

It's natural to worry, especially when your body is not as strong as it used to be before. Many older people are concerned about being physically healthy, or about getting help quickly if they fall ill. They might be concerned about being left alone if they're unable to reach the phone.

The Guardian Angel will put your mind at ease! The Angel is a simple but versatile self-support system. It will look after you and tell you (or your relatives) if anything seems to be wrong. You can also use the Angel to quickly send out alerts if you're feeling poorly. And the Angel can help you in case there's a break-in into your home, or if you're threatened in the street.

Other reasons to use an Angel might be to get your worrying relatives off your back: let them know that you're fine. Or to live a more active lifestyle, safe in the knowledge that you'll get help regardless of where you are, and what time of day it is.

The Guardian Angel is a small portable device which checks that you're safe and healthy at all times, and provides you with real-time access to help in case there is an emergency. At the core of the device are two feature sets:

- Monitoring of vital bodily signals and physical activity
- Outbound messaging which allows pre-formatted alerts to be sent to friends, relatives, and emergency services such as ambulance and police

The Angel can also record your voice and send off voice messages. Some models also come with a camera, allowing you to take photos of potential intruders or muggers. The photos are then immediately dispatched to the list of people you've defined.

The Angel is small enough to easily carry with you anywhere, and to operate it you only need to use a few simple and well-labelled buttons. Any information displayed on the screen is big and clearly legible. To send alerts, you only need to press one of the two big buttons: yellow means "I'm not well!" and red means "This is critical, please come as soon as possible".

The device also contains important medical information about you that can be used in emergencies: blood group, medication, relevant illnesses like diabetes, medical history, etc. The information can easily be accessed by emergency services.

In addition to these vital functions, of course the Guardian Angel also tells you some essential facts about your surrounding: the time, the temperature, and the weather forecast in your local area.

Finally, the Guardian Angel also provides several optional add-on services. They range from "Follow-up", which ensures that your emergency alerts lead to the necessary activity, to "Lifestyle Angel", which provides you with advice about diet and exercise, based on your physical and activity patterns.

Thomas is 48 years old, and he lives in his native Stockholm. He's been a bit concerned about his mother Brita for a while now. Brita, 74, is staying at her summer home in the Stockholm archipelago for five months every summer. Brita is insisting that she's in perfect health, and she doesn't want to move back into town before the autumn storms are whipping up huge waves in the bay outside her window. Thomas, although not the worrying type, is concerned that something might happen to his mother. She already had a minor heart attack last year, and she's not as invincible as she thinks anymore. If something would happen Brita might not be able to call for help. Even if she did, if she was unconscious by the time the emergency services would reach her, they wouldn't know about the medication she's taking. And after Thomas' father Gunnar died, there's no one there to help Brita if anything goes wrong.

When Thomas hears about the Guardian Angel, he decides that he has to get one for Brita. He buys the wristwatch Angel model for her birthday, and does some basic configuration of the Angel before he gives it to her.

Brita is initially sceptical. "You Silly Billy" she says with a smile. "I've never been healthier, and you shouldn't worry about me". However, she's secretly pleased that Thomas is concerned about her, and she promises him to use it.

When Brita has worn the Angel for a week, she's actually pretty impressed, and after a month she's addicted.

The Angel has given Brita a new sense of liberty. She's not concerned about being far away from the telephone in the house anymore, and the Angel will give her a subtle alert if she's doing things that increase her heart rate too much. She also loves the fact that she doesn't have to be by her radio at 7 pm anymore to listen to the local weather forecast – she can get it from the Angel at any point.

Brita is even showing off the Angel to other people at the island shop when she's over there. She actually meets Robert, a 68-year old single man, when discussing the Angel. They start spending time together in the summer, and after two months Robert has moved in with Brita in her summerhouse. They later on refer to that summer as "the summer of love". One evening in August, after a shopping trip to Stockholm, Brita hands over a new Angel to Robert. "It will look after you in ways that even I can't" she says.

Robert loves his Angel, and reads the manual carefully. He's into his gadgets! Robert shows Brita some functions that she wasn't even aware of, like the possibility to measure air temperature and humidity with it. Robert also convinces Brita that they both need to sign up for a simple add-on service. For an extra 20 per year, they can subscribe to the "Follow-up" service which monitors all yellow and

Mark Curtis

red alerts, and ensures that appropriate action is taken to guarantee the health and safety of the person who initiated the alert. While Robert understands the value of this service, he's a bit sceptical about the "Angel Diet" suggestions that Brita is so keen on...

Thomas is also happy with the Angel. He feels safe that if anything would be wrong with his mother he would be the first to know. He also gets weekly emails from the Angel service, ensuring him that everything is OK with Brita. The email tells him her average heart rate, blood pressure, and temperature. It also tells him how many miles she's walked that week.

After Brita and Robert have used their Angels for a year, they are informed that they have qualified for "Angel Insurance", a cheap life insurance scheme. The premiums are low because the Angel device can confirm that they are living a healthy lifestyle and are reasonably active. "Smashing!" Brian says, and applies for life insurance for both of them.

When Thomas' 14-year old daughter tells him that she's planning a back-packing trip to Italy, he realises that he would feel a lot more comfortable about her plans if she would wear an Angel. Thomas gets his daughter an Angel model that has a built-in camera. It can snap pictures of potential troublemakers and send them off to him immediately at the touch of a button. His "sell" to her is that it allows her to take cheap holiday snaps.

Could this happen? If the demand is there, it can create revenue through device sales, of data traffic revenue, add-on services and share of revenue from services offered by partners, such as life insurance. Also, governments and local authorities will be interested in the business, because it will help them optimise emergency and social support services, thereby saving costs. Much of the support and care for elderly people will be distributed from the government's social services to peer networks and relatives, relieving a big and increasing burden for the government.

Even though people might not initially want all their relatives and friends to always know their heart rate, location etc. the benefits rapidly outweigh the privacy issues. Guardian Angel is a good example of how in small but pivotal ways we may begin to trade privacy for security over time, enabled by technology. The average citizen of London is already captured 300 times a day on CCTV. We seem to have accepted this surveillance quietly as a quid pro quo for safety in the shopping centre.

It is worth repeating that this is most likely to be something we do within social networks. There are legitimate concerns that organisations will seek to take advantage of the gradual dismantling of privacy. I'd be concerned too, were it not for the fact that marketing history suggests big companies are in the main really hopeless at it, or else the evidence would be there in well targeted offers on our doormats and in-boxes.

To summarise, we are saturated in media and immersed in communications with each other. The potential for who we can be, the relationships we can have, is immense and greater than at any other time in mankind's history. Our sense of who we are as individuals, powerfully contained and created by the words we use, can and probably will change. New media play a role, allowing more to be said, more identities to be explored. It is too early to say exactly what effect this may have, though at the least it is very time consuming and confusing to manage. Uncertainty over identity has negative ramifications for levels of trust. It goes down. So will levels of privacy, as we make public essentially private stuff, and vice versa. But it may not be so bad to be observed after all, if those doing the watching are a social network you are happy to belong to.

PART TWO
The Social Potential Of New Technology

Chapter Ten
Social Networks

This chapter examines the role the cohesive role digital technology can play facilitating social networks, new and old. People do not always do the things with inventions that we imagine. The telephone was originally expected to be a device useful for playing music over distances (ironically many companies are trying to make this happen now). Where many commercial bets were made on the World Wide Web being a superb new medium for delivering content (and in some ways it is), the "killer" use turned out to be connectivity between people. Partly because of this, new scientific thinking about networks has sprung up in the last six years to explain much of how the world around us works.

Communities in cyberspace are a clear network success – we will examine why. Will that be replicated on mobile phones? Trust is the lynchpin. But trust in some of our better known social institutions is declining – what will replace them? If these trends continue – a natural conclusion is that face to face conversation will be undermined – can we detect any signs that this is happening already? Ultimately our sense of self may be changing so much that we are defined more by our web of connections, than a self-centred vision of splendid isolation.

Our space

Recently we ran a research group with 15 and 16 year old girls in London. We were discussing blogs. A blog is a personal web site featuring thoughts, photos and links to other places on the web – essentially a kind of easy to update public on-line journal. None of them had heard the term before. They understood it very quickly. What was interesting was that when we explored further their view of what you would actually *do* with a blog, their base assumption was that this was a *group* activity rather than something for individuals. They imagined a sort of communal space to which they all contributed – especially when they all finally left school. Which is in contrast to the usual view that "there is only one theme common to all (blogs): they are all about ego, about wanting to be heard".[91]

It may be contended that it's not so surprising that teenage girls – fiercely social creatures – would see a social use for this software. Yet this is also a demographic group associated with the keeping of private diaries (locked, under the bed). It is significant that the very first use they saw for blogging was to share, authored collectively. One of them said that a diary is a form of conversation.....and she'd rather have that with someone else than write it down for its own sake. We also talked about cameraphones, which some of them had. Did they bother to name the photographs? Yes, and again not for their own benefit, but with sharing at the front of their mind.

The new communications technology is extremely good at connecting together people – with each other, ideas, places. So good that distraction, as we have seen, is a major social consequence. Nonetheless the ability to connect is also its principle benefit. It has long been an axiom of the media industry that "content is king". No less a commentator than Bill Gates became fond of quoting this, as he saw the potential of the Internet reveal itself in the mid 1990's. I am not the only person to have observed that the statement "content is king" is a somewhat myopic way of viewing digital media. Never mind the difficulties of presenting content as effectively as in books, the theatre, and TV. It became clear in the early days of the Internet that *contact* was at the very least a co-sovereign with *content*.

Planet Patrol

In 1994 a far-sighted executive of drinks giant Allied Domecq, persuaded the board that they needed a strong spirit of innovation to permeate the company. Given a short rope to hang himself, Paul Wielgus and his colleague Ali Jarvis set up a project called AdVenture. They invited my colleague Mike Beeston and I to a well attended all day meeting. The purpose was to brainstorm with a number of people, internal and external, what initiatives they might undertake. Our role was to contribute "new media" thinking.

Among the themes tackled was the gay market. A persuasive theory taking hold at that time was that in some markets gay consumers were disproportionately influential in their fashion and brand choice. Drinks, especially spirits, was just such a market. If one could successfully seed a new (or even ailing) brand like Kahlua into the nightlife of the increasingly identifiable and overt gay villages in cities like London and Manchester, then a wider fashion conscious clientele may take the hint.

Recently Mike and I had seen a demonstration of some software, First Class, which provided the tools for an on-line community. It was the first time we had seen the potential for such a thing. It was not difficult to draw the conclusion that in the future there might be on-line congregations of all flavours, including gay,

Mark Curtis

communicating with each other. So we suggested that day to Allied Domecq the notion that they could build and facilitate the first Internet gay community in the UK. The advantage to the company would be that it would substantiate a claim to real involvement with a group likely to be suspicious of superficial marketing. Hosting a "sort of magazine where the readers could talk to each other, live" as we described it awkwardly (the vocabulary of the Internet was still unknown in big corporates) was likely to be a powerful statement of intent. Paul and Ali bought the idea on the spot – as soon as we described it. To date I've never known a project be approved so fast from conception.

In today's terminology First Class allowed the service designer to offer email, the ability for users to post content, run forums and live chat underneath a custom designed look and feel. We were lucky enough to find a brilliant designer and journalist, David Cook, to help us set up and then run the community. He came up with the name Planet Patrol. Set a tough deadline for launch, we worked very hard over the next few weeks to build the service. Days before it went live we were told in no uncertain terms by an "expert" that there was not enough content, and that it would fail without. David worked all hours to ensure the all-important content was there. By the time Planet Patrol launched you could use it to establish whether or not Martinique was a gay friendly destination, how to get a mortgage if you were HIV positive and where the best bars in Birmingham were. It was stuffed to the gills with content.

In a whirlwind fortnight of activity we launched by taking disks containing the software and handing them out at gay venues across the UK. At the time half the battle was to get the potential customer to dial up and use the service (most people were simply not on the web and had not heard of it) – which is why we supplied the software. Later one would have simply done it all on a web site.

Over the next year Planet Patrol became a success with 5,000 users at its peak (a huge number at that time) and a handful of media awards. But within days something else became clear. The system allowed us to monitor usage patterns very accurately. Though the "content" we had laboured over was being read, measured by what people were actually doing, it was not the most important feature by a long chalk. We had offered a community with a strong sense of its own identity a way to talk – and they grasped it with alacrity. What was popular were forums where they (via e-mail) discussed any issue under the sun, and the chat service where up to 10 users could type messages live and see the history of a discussion. The latter would typically come alive at about midnight. The stuff we had written and sourced was of course important context. Because there was lot of it, and it was about gay issues, it provided a kind of reassurance that this was a gay place. Sometimes it even sparked conversations. However we could see that content played second fiddle to connection.

It was an early lesson and as digital communications have evolved the truth of it has been borne out in numerous ways.

- eBay is a trading community: without the content and interaction provided by its participants it would be an empty husk.
- Friends Reunited has built a business out of putting people in touch with each other.
- Habbo Hotel provides teenagers with a virtual place to hang out.
- SMS took off because it provided an alternative form of communication.
- Instant messenger services likewise
- Betting exchanges have changed the betting industry by creating a market between punters

Some of Amazon's most useful features, and the ones that give it competitive edge, are those that put users in contact with each other's views. For instance if you are looking at Elvis Costello you will be offered the suggestion that "other users who bought music by Elvis Costello also bought music by these artists: David Bowie, XTC, The Kinks, Joe Jackson, Andy Partridge." Listmania offers users to the opportunity to publish their own lists based on themes such as "Must Read Political Books" or "High Fidelity – The best 20 records ever". Customer reviews (text and a starring system) provide another way to bring user written content to the surface. All of these work for the customer because they provide alternative and serendipitous ways to browse and find things – within a context where there is some assurance that precious time will not be wasted. It stems from a simple unspoken calculation: if this person likes this stuff, maybe they are similar to me, so I might like other things they enjoy.

The rise of Social Software

Currently some of the most dynamic areas of activity in digital media are based on social networks. New services such as Friendster, Orkut and LinkedIn are basing themselves entirely on social networks. Here's how Orkut describes itself:

Orkut is an online community website designed for friends. The main goal of our service is to make your social life, and that of your friends, more active and stimulating. orkut 's social network can help you both maintain existing relationships and establish new ones by reaching out to people you've never met before. Who you interact with is entirely up to you. Before getting to know an orkut member, you can even see how they're connecting to you through the friends network.

Mark Curtis

orkut makes it easy to find people who share your hobbies and interests, look for romantic connections or establish new business contacts. You can also create and join a wide variety of online communities to discuss current events, reconnect with old college buddies or even exchange cookies recipes...

If you haven't yet received an invitation to join, please be patient. We'd love to immediately include everyone who wants to participate; however, we're also trying to ensure that orkut remains a close-knit community. Over the next few weeks, hopefully, the network will grow to a point where everyone who wants to join has the opportunity to do so.

It is our mission to help you create a closer, more intimate network of friends. We hope to put you on the path to social bliss soon.

Enjoy (=

Call me a nasty old cynic but quite a few alarm bells ring when I'm offered social bliss. LinkedIn ("Your network is bigger than you think"[92]) exists at a more hard-headed end of the spectrum. The angle here is definitely business.

Linkedin is an online service helping professionals find and connect with one another more effectively. Whether looking for jobs, a lead for that next deal, or seeking out an industry expert, users can make contact with thousands of professionals through a chain of trusted connections. The company was founded by Reid Hoffman and is based in Mountain View, California.

As an executive at PayPal, Reid found himself spending much of his time connecting people. While the company grew from startup to IPO and ultimately acquisition by eBay, he was constantly bringing together various employees, customers, partners, and other contacts. The process can be time consuming and often you may be unaware of the true breadth of your network. Yet connecting people is essential to virtually all businesses, from people at large organizations operating with more independence to "free agent" workers navigating their own web of clients and collaborators.

On one occasion, Reid spent five frustrating days looking for a Flash designer. He sent emails to his connections, seeking replacements for stale email addresses, yet nobody knew anyone who was both qualified and available. The following Friday, after setting up a job requisition and starting to review resumes, a fellow exec poked

---

[92] Is it just me, or is there the faintest hint that you are being sold the network equivalent of a penile extension?

her head into Reid's cubicle. She told Reid he ought to come meet someone applying to PayPal — a Flash designer. This candidate was a friend of another PayPal employee who, completely unaware of the need for such a designer, had merely brought the friend in to meet people. Had he been able to explore his extended network of people connected to his immediate contacts, Reid's search would have been completed in hours rather than days or weeks. After leaving PayPal, Reid assembled a team to create new tools to expand and improve the ways we network.

Judging by the number of invitations I have had to join LinkedIn (from members) it has rapidly found a market and word has spread. Much of the focus is on jobs – both companies seeking employees and vice versa. The spread is impressive. At the time of writing this, LinkedIn tells me that my network is more than 910,000 people. 3,300 of those are only two links away – i.e.: they are a friend of a friend. 116,000 are two links away – a friend of a friend of a friend. If I upload my address book (which you can do) I discover another 41 people I know who already belong to LinkedIn. A network of almost 1 million seems a little unreal. To be fair, I have used Linked In professionally to search for potential recruits, and it did deliver.

All of this begs the question of trust. LinkedIn has thought of this: trust is a major theme. You can always see how many links away from someone you are, and track back to your personal network. Endorsements from other users are offered as a major feature. As yet this is not convincing: endorsements are few so the trust is established mainly by virtue of the connections being there and visible. I suspect that true trust remains an elusive creature in the digital world. LinkedIn suffers from a lack of social context: there is no binding motif for all these people to be "available" to each other, except for the sake of the network itself, driven by short term commercial needs. Actually that may be enough, as we will see when we look at the issue of "weak links" and trust later.

It remains to be seen whether LinkedIn and Orkut themselves are successful. Networks are not new. The appeal of these innovative services lies in the way they have made it so much easier to establish connections – much faster, more targeted. Through them and countless other web based social network services – especially in dating – we become direct marketers of our own skills and desires. LinkedIn operates much like a media owner capable of extraordinarily precise targeting. Its product is its users.

A problem is whether or not we can actually handle such extended networks of acquaintances. Research has shown that most people have about 12 significant others in their life: people for whom they would truly grieve for an extended time in the event of their death. The figure for numbers we claim as friends tends to average at 135. Most people cannot put names to faces for more than 2,000 or so – which is why schools tend not to be bigger than this (the head teacher will not be able to know

                                          Mark Curtis

everyone). If this is the case, then it suggests that for many of us (but not all) there are mental limits to our social networks. It is doubtful that new technology will change this. What it can do is create new opportunities to facilitate, explore and use our social networks. LinkedIn and Orkut are just the start. Evidence coming from elsewhere suggests that network thinking is becoming a leitmotiv for the 21st century.

The new science of networks

Two new books appeared in 2002 that gave scientific endorsement to this trend in thinking already manifest in tracts such as "Connexity" (Geoff Mulgan 1997) and "Emergence" (Steven Johnson 2001). Politicians were becoming aware of it too – Tony Blair's appeal to "joined-up thinking" being the best known example. The new message was that the world was more closely connected than we had previously thought or discussed. In "Linked"[93] (Albert-Laszlo Barabasi) and "Nexus" [94] (Mark Buchanan) the authors introduced new thinking, principally from the fields of pure mathematics and theoretical physics, that showed that networks are basic structures of our world and have clear underpinning rules. Both books tell the story of Stanley Milgram's legendary six degrees of separation experiment carried out in America in the 1960's. Milgram, a psychologist, set out to form a picture of the web of personal connections that make society. He sent letters to randomly chosen recipients in Wichita and Omaha. The letters revealed that they were part of a social study. They also contained the name and address and some brief information about a "target person" (in Boston). The recipient could only send the letter to the target *if they knew them.* Otherwise they were instructed to send it to someone they thought *more likely to know the target.* An acquaintance of Milgram's guessed that it might take 100 intermediates for the letters to get through. This suggested a very high likelihood that none would make it. Astonishingly it seems that 42 of the 160 letters made it (though accounts vary).[95] Even more remarkably, the average number of people who handled the letters before they reached the target was 5.5. The idea was popularised in a play (and later a film) by John Guare in1991 with the title "Six Degrees of Separation". The concept that we are all closely linked by no more than six people has passed since then into popular culture. Recently Channel 4 in the UK made a documentary from it: an English girl attempted to find a Mongolian herder whose photo she had seen in a book once. Although she failed to do it in six links,

---

[93] Perseus

[94] Norton

[95] This is the number Barabasi gives, Duncan Watts says 60 out of 300 at http://www.wired.com/wired/archive/11.06/relation_spc.html and Buchanan says only that "most of the letters eventually made it…"

---

it still only took eight. Numerous other tests of the theory have generally proved it to be true – perhaps not the exact number 5.5 but the idea that we are all socially linked much more closely than we might rationally think has stuck, and there is good evidence for it. It really is a small world.

Barabasi and Buchanan use Milgram as a starting point. They then tell the fascinating story of how in the late 1990's mathematicians such as Duncan Watts, Steve Strogatz and Barabasi himself provided proof that Milgram's results were not a freak of statistics. In fact they could have been predicted because his experiment merely provided evidence of a "small world" network. These structures are not just social or even human. According to Buchanan "social networks turn out to be nearly identical in their architecture to the World Wide Web…Each of these networks shares deep structural properties with the food webs of any ecosystem and with the network of business links underlying any nation's economic activity. Incredibly, all these networks possess precisely the same organisation as the network of connected neurons in the human brain and the network of interacting molecules that underlies the living cell…These discoveries are making a new science of networks possible…".

A defining structural feature of small world networks is that some points on any network tend to be much more connected than others. They are known as connectors or hubs. They are not hard to spot. It's the colleague who always strikes up conversation with the person next to them on a plane, and gets their card too, and bothers to e-mail them later. On the web it is places like Yahoo or Google that are superconnected by hyperlinks to and from other sites. In the world of blogging these two examples come together: very well connected bloggers both know lots of other people AND have lots of links pointing to their blogs. Topologies of the web show a very high degree of clustering (sites closely linked together around hubs). According to Barabasi "Hubs are special. They dominate the structure of all networks in which they are present, making them look like small worlds. Indeed with links to an unusually large number of nodes, hubs create short paths between any two nodes in the system. Consequently while the average separation between two randomly selected people on Earth is six, the distance between anybody and a connector is often only one or two. Similarly, while two pages on the Web are 19 clicks away, Yahoo.com, a giant hub, is reachable from most web pages in two to three clicks. From the perspective of hubs, the world is indeed very tiny."

Work by sociologist Mark Granovetter adds an intriguing twist. He has shown the importance of "weak links". In lay terms, these are casual acquaintances. They play a crucial role – and one that LinkedIn explicitly understands. If people only ever saw their close friends, their horizons, and ability to connect with other clusters of people, would be extremely limited because by definition a group would be most likely just to know its own members. However your mates do have friends who are not your close friends, some of whom you know to say hello to. These

Mark Curtis

are weak links. Granovetter showed in one study how 16% of people got new jobs though someone they saw "often", but 84% through people they saw "occasionally" or "rarely". As Buchanan summarises, "without weak ties, a community would be fragmented into a number of isolated cliques".

There is much to be said about the new science of networks – it has in my view profound implications for marketing and business in general. There is also the disturbing conclusion that it is a fundamental law of networks that the rich (hubs) get richer (more connected). This might suggest uncomfortably that the politics of redistribution is doomed to failure if its objective is a levelling of society. It also lends credence to the old saying that what matters is who you know not what you know.

Why networks now?

Three developments of the last thirty years fertilised the ground for network thinking.

They are the growth in ecology studies, the challenge to reductionism from systemic thinking and the arrival of the Internet.

Inspired by writers such as Frijtof Capra (The Web of Life, The Hidden Connections), Rachel Carson (Silent Spring) and James Lovelock (Gaia), the ecology movement has penetrated public consciousness. We are now very aware of the concept that life on earth is a complex system that can be considered as a single organism. This more sophisticated awareness of the environment stimulates us to think of all things as interdependent because there is now overwhelming evidence that changes in one part of the system create unexpected but related transformations elsewhere. This philosophy directly informs the new network thinking. For instance Steven Johnson draws repeatedly on organic examples in Emergence (from ant colonies to the delightfully named slime mold). Barabasi and Buchanan illustrate network theory repeatedly with examples drawn from nature: an oceanic food web, river systems, snowflakes, yeast.

The ecology movement is closely linked to a major shift in scientific thinking: the move from reductionist thinking to looking at systems as a whole. From the enlightenment until recently most scientific research focused on examining phenomena in ever increasing detail. As Barabasi says, the idea was that "to comprehend nature…we first must decipher its components…therefore for decades we have been forced to see the world through its constituents. We have been trained to study atoms and superstrings to understand the universe; molecules to comprehend life; individual genes to understand complex human behaviour…". But now we understand so many of the pieces, the big picture remains elusive. "The reason is simple: riding reductionism, we run into the hard wall of complexity…nature is not a well-designed puzzle with only one way to fit it back together…today we increasingly recognise that nothing happens in isolation." This is why pattern recognition and chaos theory have become such hot topics.

Systemic thinking and ecological awareness created the pre-conditions for network theory – and the Internet was the catalyst that galvanised its appearance in academic circles. As it grew at a remarkable rate, the organisation of this new network became a natural area of study. Could it be mapped? Why did it behave in the way it did? Were there underpinning rules? Why was Google successful? It is surely not a coincidence that it was in late 1998 that academics began to make significant breakthroughs in charting territory which had opened up only a few years before.

So we have seen that much of the success of new communications technology has been driven by connecting people together. We've also seen that the Internet both provided outstanding examples of network rules in action, and the impetus for new network thinking to break cover. What kind of social networks flourish digitally? Do communities work by the same rules in the physical world, on the web and over phones?

Digital community

In recent work with my colleagues we've taken a long look at communities and developed a model for thinking about they way they work, to help us identify what kind of social networks will work well in different circumstances. We identified four building blocks all of which have to be in place for communities to develop. They are:

Need – the basic drive (push) we all feel to varying degrees to belong and interact

Context – the circumstances (pull) that trigger and sustain participation

Linkage – the contact made between members of the community

Usage – the result of time and frequency of interaction in the community

The dynamics of this system are complicated by the fact that people have different reasons (needs) to join and participate in a community. These are:

*the need to **belong*** – often communicated by a nod, smile or pleasantry, the need to belong is a basic driver, a bedrock for many communities and an entry point for many

*the need to **share*** – a step forward from belonging, we need to share interests (such as football) and themes (such as conflict in the Middle East) with other people who are like-minded

Mark Curtis

*the need to **bond*** – here we refer to a deeper and more meaningful level of sharing, as for example in families or between close friends, which touches people and is a clear sign that social capital is evident in the community

*the need to **help** or be helped* – this need is self explanatory and is evidenced by communities that provide mutual self help (e.g. online gaming or hacker communities) or support for others (e.g. rotary clubs)

How these needs are expressed can be good or bad, constructive or destructive. The model does not discriminate. Nor does the model force people (or their communities) to identify with just one of the needs. The same person or the same community can experience different needs at the same time and over time. The model simply points to different reasons for joining and participating. A good example is the National Childbirth Trust in the UK. Expectant parents join usually on the basis that they need to share understanding of what they are about to go through and perhaps learn. If they get on well with the other parents, then bonding becomes evident through informal events (come round for tea) and language or symbols ("our group"). Finally the group may provide practical help to each other through babysitting.

The NCT is an example drawn from the physical world of parents and babies. Looking at digital technologies, it is interesting to see where different media are strong or weak at supporting social networks.

The Internet is very good at meeting the needs of **sharing** and **helping**, less good (yet) at making people feel they **belong** or getting them to **bond**. The best example of sharing is of course p2p file sharing which has so massively disrupted the music industry. Take also the countless discussion groups that exist on the web to talk about football or politics. In the main, contributors are sharing views or information but the medium makes it hard to achieve real bonding. In the physical world bonding normally becomes evident when stories are told (hey! remember the time that Micky pretended to be Brad Pitt!) or symbols exchanged (e.g.: we all wear the same T-shirt). The relative brevity of most postings means that true bonding on the web is rare. Nonetheless the Internet allows people to trawl much wider and deeper for "people like me" than they can possibly do in real life. Yet the medium hides a lot of personal context: "on the Internet no-one knows you are a dog". People like me tends to be defined mainly by interest (trainspotting) not a richer set of pointers such as accent, age. The converse of this is that digital allows trans boundary work more easily – people with different pieces of the puzzle can collaborate more easily. So helping is also well facilitated on-line: anyone who has asked a question of a technical nature to a user group will know quite how helpful these can be. The breadth of the pool available means that help can be surprisingly easy and cheap (if not free) to come by: the Internet dramatically lowers transaction costs. However the price is that once again the stickiness (the degree to which members feel bound to the community) is weak: the social price of withdrawing from, or withholding help, is likely to be low.

Lack of stickiness is why the Internet is not great at satisfying people's need to belong. Arguably this could be met just through a visit to a web site. I may feel part of the Chelsea fans community (if I wish to) without registration or contribution. I can get a feel for the on-line Buddhist community without any commitment or exposure. My mental context can be idle interest (it's free and easy to find communities) or genuine need to know. But no-one (except the server) knows that I am there. Anonymity and the proliferation of choice means there has to be more. Another difference is that multiple identities can be so easily adopted which rather undermines belonging too.

Mobile community

The mobile phone exhibits different characteristics as a facilitator of social networks. The most obvious point is that it is considerably less anonymous in its current form (everyone knows they can be identified by their number, and some people know that they can be identified by place too). In a small way mobile phones do satisfy the need to **belong** through ringtones and logos. Younger people in particular use these to send clear signals to their peers: look at me, I fit in. Of course sometimes the reverse is true and the desired message is about standing out from the crowd,

At first sight the mobile is not a good **sharing** medium for communities – fine of course for one to one, but not great when more people are involved. Screen size limitations make it hard to replicate the success that forums have had on the web because it is harder to establish context and track back through conversations to see what is being discussed and who has contributed. But this may be a limited view of sharing. The rise of "personal content" (see next chapter) actually makes phones a very interesting medium for communal sharing, either for capturing stuff (taking photos for instance) or reviewing it. Digital Graffiti[96] is a great example of the potential for sharing communities to use the mobile in a location sensitive context.

The immediacy and personal nature of the phone lends itself well to **bonding**. As the phone is more personal than the coldness of the Internet it is likely to be a better bonding route – especially if voice is made an integral or optional part of a service. In some communities, there could be an implicit path from text, to text plus visuals, to voice, to meeting. Customers are almost certainly going to be prepared to pay more for bonding than sharing or belonging.

---

[4] See chapter 3

Mark Curtis

Lastly mobile has a role to play when **helping** is the key community driver. Again the insistent immediacy of the device makes it better than the Internet for time critical help and the motivation both to ask and receive via the phone is strong and habitual. Likely to be time critical, mobile help could also be location specific (e.g.: community traffic news). Too many demands being placed on a community could be an issue, intrusive and hard to deal with. People will expect controls to be applied either centrally or on the device.

The Internet has shown how vigorous communities can be when mediated by new technology, especially when used to share or help. Mobile maybe even more of a community medium. It does not take models like the one above to know that people use mobile to stay in touch with their friends and colleagues.

Yet there are some big blockers to work round for mobile social networks to really be a success.

- Reasons to join, reason to stay

"Real Life" communities are easy to find. A lot of the time we simply live in them – at school, at work, the gym. So are web communities – which are often placed next to their context (a discussion forums on a newspaper web site about some hot news) or to a portal (such as Yahoo) or can be found by a search engine. These factors are not givens on mobile devices. People are more likely to discover mobile community tools through real life social networks or possibly as extensions of web communities. Screen size limitations also mean the full structure and content of a mobile social network is likely to be less apparent than in physical or web based communities. In other words, you can't see it in one glance, like you can all the people at a party. This limitation on context is going to have to be addressed as much as possible through design. For instance by finding ways to communicate graphically, showing the popularity or level of energy in a community, and by making active community threads as visible as possible. Even then, users will need and probably expect a high degree of focus in the content. The handheld device is an unforgiving place to waste people's time.

- Hierarchy of needs

Mobile communities will need the tools to progress from belonging to sharing, bonding and helping. These tools should enable profiles (who am I), filtering (who am I happy to talk to, what about and when), security (keeping it in the club), and search (make it easy to find things) so that users feel able to move to a more complex level of interaction. An interesting sign that users have progressed may be a demand for text that is enriched by symbols, like smileys but beyond! Maybe these symbols will initially be seeded by service providers, but tools should also be provided to enable symbols to emerge or be created by users.

- Content

Mobiles are poor devices (though getting better) for originating and consuming content, especially text. It's hard to type a lot on a typical keypad. On the other hand, the mobile is convenient and always on – which makes it a good device for receiving if not consuming content. This implies that communication is likely to be in small packages, including voice and photos. It is also probable that the PC should be seen as a symbiotic partner in providing tools for generating and consuming content.

- Cost

Participation in a mobile community will cost money. This is less the case in the real world or the web. This means that social networks will only use mobile tools when they play to the medium's competitive benefits – it's personal, convenient and always on. These benefits work especially well for people who use the mobile to bond and payment then is less likely to be an issue.

- Trust

Mobiles are more personal and less anonymous than PC's. This engenders trust but also vulnerability. To address the latter, people will want to manage their identity (easily and simply), be able to filter inbound messages and impose sanctions if necessary – the more so if the community is likely to be bonding or helping. Transparent rules are prerequisite and there may be a need to guarantee security and privacy and to build-in trust mechanisms such as peer reviews and ratings.

As these issues are addressed – and they will be – so mobile will take its place alongside the Internet in giving more opportunities for social networks to form, evolve and interact. Of all the barriers listed above, lack of trust is the biggest and most difficult to overcome for the potential of new media to be fulfilled.

Trust

As we have seen earlier, it is not entirely true that distance has died. The distance lent by being a long way away, or because your identity is hidden, lowers responsibility; bluntly it's a lot more tempting to hurl insults at someone if you know it's hard for them to send round their big brother. Hence "flaming" or out of control abuse became a well-known early phenomenon on the Internet. Because distance is still real, a true sense of belonging can be fragile.

If social networks are to thrive in a digital environment, sooner or later you have to be able to trust those people with whom you interact. This is critical or we fail to build social capital. Trust is an invisible form of social capital. An emergent response on the Web has been to build engines of trust on some very specific sites, and we can expect to see many more of these. They work by getting users to rate each other. The best example is eBay, a market where trust is crucial to the smooth flow of commerce. Feedback ratings give a clear sense of how honest and efficient a seller has been. As they grow over time, they also have the happy consequence of tightening loyalty to eBay and therefore the community. Slashdot.org, a web community that goes under the banner of "news for nerds" evolved a very sophisticated system for developing trust. Steven Johnson describes it thus "If you've spent more than few sessions as a registered Slashdot user, the system may on occasion alert you that you have been given moderator status (not unlike a jury summons arriving in your in-box). As in the legal analogy, moderators only serve for a finite stretch of time, and during that stretch they have the power to rate contributions made by other users, on a scale of –1 to 5. But that power diminishes with use: each moderator is endowed only with a finite number of points that he or she can distribute by rating user contributions. Dole out all your ratings and your tenure as a moderator comes to an end."[97] Complicated but clever, the point is to cut the crap and allow the reader to filter their reading through a communal judgement, cross referenced to ensure that the moderators are rated too. Slashdot has provided a digital answer to the question 'who guards the guards?'.

Authority transformed

If we can get these engines of collaboration right, it could be that in the future we place more trust in such social networks than in traditional authority. Michael Willmott and William Nelson believe that we are already witnessing what they call "the personalisation of authority".[98] Their theory is that trust in traditional institutions is waning, and quite fast. Research done in 1997 and 2001 by the Future Foundation showed that newspapers, TV, government, political parties and business leaders have all declined when rated as 'sources of influence' over individual's views on social and environmental issues. In contrast family, friends and work colleagues have increased slightly. It seems like we are turning more to our social networks to explore the opinions we hold. Willmott and Nelson predict that "this personalisation

---

[97] Emergence
[98] Complicated Lives – Wiley

of authority allows people to define their own networks of authority" and that this "is encouraging more contact and connectivity directly between individuals – something that is aided by, and encouraging, the new communications technologies". As a result "who one's contacts are – who one can trust and rely upon for good advice – becomes more important. The connections you have and the capabilities and influence of your friends and families – your 'social capital' – becomes critical."

Enabled by technology, this trend will take some surprising and radical forms. In 2001 we developed just such a concept that came within a squeak of changing authority. One sunny August afternoon we were talking about two interesting but seemingly unrelated observations. The first was that voting on reality TV shows such as Big Brother had handed a degree of real control to the audience. The second was that the stock market almost always outperforms expert fund managers, formed as it is by the aggregate decision making of millions of investors. In other words (and unsurprisingly when you think about it) the market knew better than the highly paid analysts.[99] So we asked, where else might this be the case? Where might control be better vested in the crowd? Could new technology play a role?

It only took a couple of seconds to think of football. Who was to say that the manager of a football club knew better than 40,000 fans in the stands? Why not let them vote on who should play in the team each week? After all, as anyone who has been to a game knows, a crowd makes its feelings known audibly about team selection and substitutions during the run of play.

Of course we knew immediately that no big club would let us do this. But we also realised that if we could persuade a smaller club to experiment in a less threatening way, it might make a great reality TV programme. And the involvement of TV might persuade the club…

A club was found – Stevenage Borough – residents of the Nationwide League (semi-professional and one level below Division Three), with an average home gate of below 3,000. The manager, Paul Fairclough, was far-sighted and imaginative enough to see the potential. Cautiously, and with his eye firmly on revenue, the Chairman agreed. A draft format was evolved which suggested that three positions each week should be up for the vote, the manager would select the rest of the team. The TV show would present the choices to viewers and expert analysis of the players' form. Then the viewers would choose using text or interactive TV voting. Discussions would take place on a web forum. On Saturdays the fans could demand substitutions by SMS after 20 minutes: if more than 50% of the home crowd insisted a player came off, then he would. The choice of replacement rested with the manager on the touchline.

---

[99] This theory has recently been boosted by James Surowiecki in "The Wisdom of Crowds: Why the Many Are Smarter Than the Few and How Collective Wisdom Shapes Business, Economies, Societies and Nations" - Doubleday

Mark Curtis

So we went to Channel 4, where they loved the idea, and after some discussion commissioned the programme in less than three months. It was to be called "You're the Manager" and a production company (Lion) was drafted in to refine the programme ideas and make it. Filming began. The rushes were great. For a while it did look like we were going to introduce a completely new idea to sport. Then with two weeks to go before the first programme, the publicity broke.

There were two types of reaction. Ordinary football fans were very supportive. The idea of having a real say in the running of a club you loyally spend hundreds or thousands of pounds to support each year was and is very appealing. The football authorities were much less enamoured of the project. A very senior figure in English football was adamant that he would never let this or anything like it happen. The buffoonish Gordon Taylor, Chief Executive of the Professional Footballers Association insisted loudly that it would undermine the professionalism of the game. What I think he meant was that it undermined the traditional power structures of the game. And a lot of people found that hard to accept. The Conference league decided not to allow filming to go ahead on their grounds after all, which killed the project. A Conference spokesman said: "The presentation from Channel 4 was very impressive and extremely professional. However we do not consider that the best interests of all 22 member clubs would be served if we allowed this proposal to go ahead. Football is a mix of sport and entertainment and it is our opinion that this proposal took away the sporting element and left only the entertainment." Naturally, letting fans have a voice would hardly be sporting would it?

Two years later we still meet people who remember the almost-programme and usually say the same thing – "oh yes – that was surely an idea whose time will come". The point of the story is this: digital media could be very powerful if they fulfill their potential to shift authority away from the establishment and towards social networks. Expect more ideas that make you the manager.

Face to face

There is a darker side to all of this: if we rely more on electronic media to participate in society, will face to face interaction decline? We have seen already how rich face to face interaction can be, with all the non-verbal gesticulations and clues we throw out. Perhaps some people will retort that it does not matter if we have less face to face and more machine mediated interaction. We should certainly beware not to romanticise a transaction which often lets us down (I'm thinking of various experiences with bank managers). But most normal people will recognise that something important and ineffably human could be lost, or at least diminished by such a trend.

Actually it is not clear that such a trend is taking place. Evidence in favour might seem to come from the UK's Office for National Statistics which reported in 2004 a doubling of the number of people working from home some of the week (now 8 million) over 1997. 2.1 million work from home full-time. In 2001 15% of workers in a survey claimed to use home Internet access for work, and around 17% of workers used the Internet at work to access personal stuff.[100] It is believed that the increased availability of broadband and the pressures of commuting have combined to drive the numbers up suddenly, after years of predictions that it would eventually happen. So it seems likely that working some or all of the week from home means that workers will see less of their colleagues and customers – even if they can communicate with them over e-mail, phone and video conferencing.

But a key driver for home working is also desire to spend more time face to face with your family. According to a report by Abbey National and the Future Foundation the overwhelming majority of us believe we are spending more time than our parents did in various activities with our children. Cutting out commuting is one immediate way we can gain that time. So perhaps we are trading one kind of face for another.

Then again, some commentators think that children too will spend more time at home, less at a building called school, because they will be at school at home. According to Susan Greenfield[101] about 150,000 children in the UK currently do this, and this number is predicted to treble by 2010. IT makes possible a much more effective and flexible curriculum at home, and even the possibility of interaction with pupils and teachers from different cultures, far away. But "the problem with an IT-based education, with the focus on the individual going at their own pace for their own individual needs and curiosities, is that surely there will be an inevitable loss of direction in terms of what we are learning as a cohesive society."

She goes further and fantasises about a future where conversations are augmented by technology so heavily, that eventually mankind prefers the mediated kind. Face to face becomes something you do for novelty… "It has become a kind of hobby, a little like camping without electricity or running water used to be way back in the twentieth century. First you have to enter the 'natural room' and take off all IT embedded and smart clothing. You then sit in a solid, non-smart chair that will never change its function, form or colour, and unless you have made a prior arrangement, you have to wait until another person feels the 'natural' urge. The next step is to have a face-to-face dialogue, in real time. Your generation finds this activity very frustrating, After all, it is impossible to access information for reference quickly, and you have needed to memorise very little for other aspects of daily life. What is there to talk about using just your own isolated brain? And even if you did

---

[100] From M-commerce, a Future Foundation report, quoted in Complicated Lives.
[101] In "Tomorrow's People"

Mark Curtis

have a way of harnessing whatever facts you might need, what would be the point of this random, slow, capricious interchange with another person? What could they tell you and why would you want to know it? It's all too lonely, too slow, and takes too much proactive effort. Yet your grandparents still seem to enjoy this primitive activity…". Note that Greenfield's vision encompasses many of the themes we are looking at. The subject finds 'natural' interaction too slow, and lonely! Distraction, in this vignette, has taken over completely.

For the time being, this remains Futurology (and to be fair the author is only presenting it as one possible outcome). I have come across no compelling evidence that face to face human interaction is declining. Yet more than any other generation so far, today's toddlers will grow up seeing their parents and role models spending large portions of their life interacting through screens and handsets. Sociologist Robert Putnam showed in "Bowling Alone" how social impact can be stored up and only become evident years after a generation's mores have been formed. If adults spend more time interacting with screens of one kind or another, what will the next generation regard as normal? What sense of self does it communicate?

People of the network

In an article in Time Magazine in 2000, digital commentator Kevin Kelly coined the phrase "people of the screen". He distinguished this group from those he called "People of the Book. These are the good people who make newspapers, magazines, the doctrines of law, the offices of regulation and the rules of finance. They live by the book, by the authority derived from authors, and are centered at the power points of New York City and Washington. The foundation of this culture is ultimately housed in texts. They are all on the same page, so to speak.

On the other side (and on an axis that runs through Hollywood and Redmond, Wash.) we have the People of the Screen. The People of the Screen tend to ignore the classic logic of books; they prefer the dynamic flux of the screen. Movie screens, TV screens, computer screens, Game Boy screens, telephone screens, pager screens and Day-Glo megapixel screens we can only imagine today, plastered on every surface."

These distinctions are perhaps to be superceded by a third and in the long term more penetrating one – people of the network. According to a recent report by Mintel, 25% of primary school children in the UK use a mobile. The numbers of 7 to 10 year olds with a mobile phone has almost doubled in three years. Another report in November 2003[102] showed that 96% of 15 – 24 year olds own a mobile phone. It also suggested that many of them would feel socially isolated if they were

---

[102] Roar/Channel 4

deprived of the phone or unable to get on the Internet for a fortnight. An expensive bill was a sign of social status, a sure marker of popularity.

In a way that old fashioned dog eared address books never could, the panoply of modern communications reveal to us our social networks in all their glory. Think of all the ways we see our networks. A single person may be able to view their network from the following angles:

A buddy list on a messenger service
An e-mail address book
Contacts listed on their phone
Contacts listed on their sim card
Their e-mail in-box
Their e-mail sent box
Missed calls on their phone
Received calls on their phone
Their SMS in-box
The address book of their personal organiser such as a Palm
Forums they participate in on-line
An intranet directory of people at work

None of these were standard for the majority even 10 years ago. (Indeed right now there is much speculation that social software will come to TV, which will allow viewers to understand which of their friends are watching the same programmes as them, and communicate with them while they are viewing. Imagine a kind of TV focussed Instant Messenger on the big screen in your living room. Or all of that even on your mobile (possibly more likely given that that much of what is needed is already in phones, and the TV bit is coming shortly.)[103]

When a phone is stolen, the chief concerns of most people are now not the replacement cost in money, but the effort required to rebuild their contacts book and the loss forever of sentimental text messages.

It is not surprising then, that a great deal of effort is being put into the visualisation of social networks. Designers and technologists are experimenting with different ways of mapping. Pioneering work by Valdis Krebs can be seen at www.orgnet. com. He calls it "Social Network Analysis" and claims it is "a mathematical methodology for *connecting the dots* – using science to fight terrorism. Connecting multiple pairs of dots soon reveals an emergent *network* of organization. Once you have a network map, you can measure parts of the network, or the whole, using social net-

---

[103] www.plasticbag.org and www.corante.com

Mark Curtis

work metrics." Microsoft's Social Computing Group are looking hard at this too via a "Personal Map…the goal of the Personal Map is to help users organize their email contacts in a meaningful way, based on their email behavior, without users having to provide any additional information. The Personal Map models the users social network (who they care about and their informal groups) based on communication behaviour such as who they email the most and who they email together."

For individuals, it is not yet clear exactly where the usefulness of social network mapping lies. I pretty much know who I contact frequently and who I do not. Do I need a graphic representation to show me in colour? But this is not the point: the effort being made is symptomatic of a global consciousness that personal networks are increasingly important. It has been called by one group of academics "networked individualism".[104] When you sent a letter or made a call fifteen years ago, it was to a place. A letter without a physical address could usually not be delivered. The phone you dialled rang in a place where theoretically anyone could answer it. In the mobile age you ring a person, confident that they will answer. In the e-mail age you direct your correspondence to a person not a building. As Netlab puts it "the person has become the portal. This shift facilitates *personal communities* that supply the essentials of community separately to each individual: support, sociability, information, social identities, and a sense of belonging. The person, rather than the household or group, is the primary unit of connectivity…In effect, the Internet and other new communication technology are helping each individual to personalise his or her own community. This is neither a *prima facie* loss nor gain in community, but rather a complex, fundamental transformation in the nature of community."

Organisations are beginning to think about how the network view of thick and thin connections between people can be useful. A Finnish company, Xtract, are marketing clever software that allows a mobile operator to identify social hubs and match their behaviour against other kinds of activity – such as usage of the mobile Internet. If you want to market a mobile Internet service, these are the best people to market to because they are both active users and socially influential.

Why is an increased emphasis on social networks important? It has been observed by many writers[105] in varying ways that there are three kinds of behaviour in life – dependence, independence and interdependence. The first (dependence) is a characteristic of childhood – and many people never really move beyond it. In this stage we rely on or expect others to look after us. At heart people like this believe that the world happens to them. A tell-tale sign is that dependent individuals will use the word *they* in a context such as "*they* won't let me". It is not always clear who they are. The second (independence) is where we make our decisions, and take

---

[104] Netlab at www.ascusc.org/jcmc/vol8/issue3/wellman.html
[105] A good example is Stephen Covey in "7 Habits of Highly Effective People" Free Press

responsibility for looking after ourselves. These people believe they happen to the world. Margaret Thatcher famously encouraged Britons to be more like this. It can however be a recipe for selfishness (Thatcher, in a much quoted soundbite (actually taken out of context) claimed that there is no such thing as society). The third behaviour is informed by a belief in interdependence. This is where we believe we can achieve more together than as individuals, and understand implicitly that we are indeed all linked in a system. Many people conclude that interdependent thinking is the best forward for mankind. As Alan Moore, co-author of "Communities Dominate Brands"[106] points out – "nobody is as smart as everybody".

In case this sounds like dewy-eyed utopian thinking, it should be pointed out that an increased focus on human networks will not necessarily be a social leveller. Indeed it may simply shift power even more towards people who know people. Commentator Douglas Rushkoff points out: "Increasingly the power and agency of individuals is defined not by what they know – not what's on the hard drive – but who and what they have access to – who is in their date book or how readily they can find a link…even those individuals lucky enough to be valued for their opinions and assessments will increasingly be judged by the breadth of access they have to information."[107]

However with its enormous power to reveal and facilitate social networks, digital technology can play a very positive role helping to foster a new spirit of mutuality. It is not a universal panacea – terrorists form social networks and use technology to organise. Thankfully most humans are not terrorists, and can and will turn to more positive collaboration. We have seen earlier how our sense of self can and does change, and that we will probably be prepared to trade privacy for security and co-operation. We have seen how our private sphere is becoming more public. As we increasingly see ourselves as nodes on our networks so we will begin to define ourselves more and more by the networks we operate in, made manifest by design and technology. Perhaps not everyone will find this a happy prospect but deep trends in science and society suggest it is inevitable. Better this than a fragmented world of extreme and selfish individualism. The power of the network is apparent: it is up to us to ensure that it is turned to good social purpose. For this, we may have to rethink some entrenched personal habits of behaviour.

---

[106] Futuretext 2005

[107] The Feature: www.thefeature.com 28/06/2004. In a counter balance to the view that we now all think that who you know is more important than what you know, the Henley Centre has identified a trend in the UK towards self improvement; for instance evening classes have grown dramatically, and the number of adult learning opportunities doubled between 1995 and 2001. Book clubs are growing: there are now about 50,000 in the UK. Perhaps it is both,

Mark Curtis

PART TWO
The Social Potential Of New Technology

Chapter Eleven
Adapting Our Behaviour

It is time to look at what we ourselves can do. This chapter begins to explore how we might have to change the way we approach life to take account of the new technologies that we are embracing. This is not new – technological change always requires social readjustment.

How do we deal with lots of messages arriving for us through multiple channels? We will probably need to discipline ourselves not to be distracted. This may not be so easy as discipline comes hard to modern humans. I suggest some ways we can start in our daily lives. At the core of this will be locating and growing the discipline to manage better our time, especially where it intersects with our use of technology. Knowing how and when to disengage from intense connectivity is going to be a crucial human skill. A good start will be to routinely create space for isolating ourselves from the flak of electronic communication. Ironically technology might help with this – after all it is meant to be our servant not master. We may even begin to place a premium on physical space and time that is completely disconnected.

Most people will not wish simply to become "nodes" on the "network". We need to explore how digital communication can enhance our sense of individuality and self worth, and yet learn to feel responsibility for the actions we take in a world that is linked so much more closely.

As for individuals, so too for organisations and society as a whole. Organisations will have to learn new habits. If we accept that distraction technology is a part of life – what should companies do to take account of this in the way they interact with their stakeholders?

One will be to get used to being more open, less secret. They may have no choice. They will also have to figure out how to listen to all kinds of people, and demonstrate that listening too. Again, I suggest some ways how.

Overall society may have to counter the tendency towards immediacy and re-embrace the distant view. Can we now begin to build and think long term? If the desire for immediacy is endemic in society, can we build values that place renewed emphasis on the difficult project, the vision whose promise may not be fulfilled in our lifetimes? After all, we still draw inspiration from people in the past who have done so. All this requires responsibility, and the greatest need is to accept that we all have to deal with the challenges confronting us now. Moaning that technology is providing multiple sources of distraction is not good enough: we need to take responsibility for the problem. If I am right, and communication levels in the 21st century are becoming unsustainable, we must find strategies for mental and emotional survival, and soon.

Early adopters

We are distracted by technology, and what it can do, as a subject all of its own. So much so that in the world of marketing those people most likely to be distracted first have a collective name all of their own – "early adopters". Many companies target them with innovation strategies (often erroneously in my view). They are the people thought to be most likely to buy a new piece of kit when they see or hear about it. Such exposure to novelty is made more probable by the new device pages that appear in every newspaper and many magazines now. Whole racks in newsagents are given over to magazines (Stuff, T3, Nuts) partly or totally devoted to the exploration of distraction technologies. The relentless quest for profit drives companies to innovate in this field endlessly. Take portable music as an example: we've moved from the Walkman to the CD Walkman to MiniDiscs to iPods in the space of not much more than 20 years. The drive to put music on mobile phones means this particular cycle of change is not remotely over, as the next step[108] will be to download music "over the air", that is wirelessly to the device in your hand.

Technology is offering us ever more choices, especially in communication. We now have to learn how to make and manage those choices. That negotiation is with us already: it is going on now, even as I write, and you read.

Incoming fire

Learning how to deal with over abundant communication is not easy. Research in 2004 by the University of Surrey found that more than half of those surveyed thought it was bad form to use IT equipment of any kind while in a meeting or talking to someone at work. Over 80% thought it was rude to send or look at text messages while with others.[109] If this is the case then what we think is good behaviour

---

[108] Available already but not widely adopted, yet

[109] Quoted by BBC News Online 3 June 2004. The survey contended that levels of stress in the office are increased by communications technology, because it tries patience all round. Professor Michael Warren said "We become stressed and impatient when we can't reach someone, yet we resent distractions and can become angry when we are interrupted by the mobile phone…I'm afraid the research shows we can't have our cake and eat it".

(in theory), is not what we do (in practice). Looking back over the last ten years I can trace my own responses, good and bad. During the 1990's, as volumes of e-mail grew, so I found myself changing my behaviour. At first it was a novelty, to be glanced at now and then in the off chance that someone had sent me a mail. As the odds increased that new messages would be waiting in my in-box, so I began to check its contents more frequently. At the time it never occurred to me to analyse why I did this: if someone had asked me I would probably have replied that it was in case something urgent was there. I now realise that there is ALMOST NEVER anything truly urgent in an e-mail inbox. A wise acquaintance once taught me that a useful question to ask when life throws stressful situations at you, is 'what is the worst thing that could happen in this situation?' Usually the answer turns out to be nothing so very bad after all. The same is true of e-mail: not reading it rarely turns out to be a genuine problem.

At the time I did not see this. By 2000 I was receiving about 200 e-mails a day. On return from a fortnight's holiday it could take up to two days to clear the back-log. By then I was also using a mobile as my chief telephone (I was travelling a lot). Most days it would ring several times per hour. Because Razorfish was global, and so was my job, the hours that it rang extended well into the evening (I've found that Americans in particular have an under-developed sense of international time zones). One day I found myself discussing this with a colleague and realised to my horror that some part of me was proud of the volume of correspondence I was receiving. Digging deeper, I uncovered the discomforting idea that I thought it told me (in a very rudimentary way) that I was important. When I heard other people make similar boasts I began to question whether this was a valid measurement of self-worth. In fact it made me feel more than a bit foolish.

I began to observe other issues. Messages unopened bothered me. They seemed to represent incomplete tasks. Tackling them (opening, replying, storing, deleting) gave me a sense of achievement, made me feel like I was doing my job. In a sense I was – by this stage a large part of the job did involve reading and responding to mails, picking up the phone and taking calls. But there are associated risks. Not only does dealing with mail confer an imagined sense of achievement because one can see it has gone from the screen, it is often much easier than the effort of conversing with someone. I began to think that at times maybe I was prioritising digital communication over face to face. Moreover reading and responding to mail was the first thing I liked to do in the morning. Yet I also knew that to be effective it is better to start the day with the job you least want to do – which in my work might have been a difficult conversation or composing a complex document. In comparison to these, mail was easy and I could say to myself 'well done – you've cleared your inbox – now you can get on with rest of the day'.

However, as we have seen, we are now 'always on'. Digital communication is potentially always arriving. Thus a bad habit of the morning could extend right across the day. I could always prioritise messages over meetings.

Then one day I was leading a meeting with a very well known technology company. An agreement had been made globally that Razorfish should partner with them. Our meeting was to discuss how this would work in practice in Europe. During the usual hiatus at the start while coffee was made and people settled down, all the people from the partner company opened their laptops, plugged into the Internet (in our meeting room) and began to check their mail. Which was fine, except they continued to do so after the meeting had begun. Some of them were taking and sending text messages too, one actually had whispered phone conversations on his mobile. Not only was this completely dysfunctional behaviour, it was making it very hard to conduct a focussed event. I decided to make it clear that this had to stop in the interests of good, clear communication – so asked that everyone switch off their mobiles and shut down their laptops. This did not make me popular. In fact I had to repeat the request several times to the phone whisperer, with increasing insistence, until he reluctantly complied.

Telling this tale now I realise that for many familiar with big (and some small) corporations it will not come as a surprise – though it would surely be a huge shock to an executive time traveller from 15 years ago. Since then I have seen the same behaviour in many instances – often in very well disciplined companies.[110] Perhaps it is endorsed and encouraged by those at the top. A friend of mine who works in an IT services company says it happens all the time. He also observed that the cause is often people being in the wrong meetings.[111] Stuck in a dull meeting, if someone decides that they have nothing to contribute or learn, then it is tempting to turn to other tasks if the opportunity is there. The answer to that problem is surely to ensure that people don't waste time attending pointless meetings. This of course is an age old organisational conundrum, and not the fault of new communication technologies. One might argue that it is better for them to use time answering mail than pretending to participate. However what of those people who go to meetings, but decide that only bits of the day are relevant. Can they too selectively duck out until the time is right to pay attention? How do they know which bits to listen to? And what of the signals this sends to other participants?

Charles Handy in "The Hungry Spirit"[112] tells of the head of a large consult-

---

[110] It is likely that in some cases the behaviour is also a form of power language: the message being sent is "you are neither important nor relevant to me, therefore I'm focussing on something else". This message is powerfully reinforced by the physical barrier erected by a laptop screen.

[111] Ironically the tools of e-mail and digital diaries have made it easier to organise meetings and invite a wider selection of attendees – I suspect (but have no evidence) that this has lead to more pointless meetings in the last 10 years.

[112] Arrow

Mark Curtis

ing group who complained to him that "her people are now spending so much time listening, reading and responding to their incoming communications that they have ceased to think. Efficient? Yes. Effective? I'm not so sure". Actually I'd question the efficiency too.

Discipline

Obviously we do not all live lives where corporate meetings and constant e-mail form part of the landscape. Yet, if we widen the scope of distraction to include all the new technologies in all parts of our lives, for many people the fundamental question will be familiar. How do we change our behaviour to cope?

The first answer feels very unsophisticated but presents a big challenge to society and individuals. It is that we need to build a stronger sense of discipline and self control into our daily lives.

Discipline is a theme that has been central to the writings of some of the most influential social and business commentators of the last 25 years. In "The Road Less Travelled",[113] psychotherapist M. Scott Peck describes discipline as the set of tools we need to deal with the fact that "life is difficult" and always constitutes a series of problems to be grappled with rather than ignored. If this message strikes some as rather old-fashioned, perhaps that is because he is dealing in universal issues, familiar to all ages.

Peck wrote before the digital era (in 1979), but reading his book now it is hard not to be struck by how relevant his analysis is to the issues of distraction technology. For instance his four discipline "tools" are:

- Delaying gratification
- Acceptance of responsibility
- Dedication to truth
- Balancing

We have seen how immediacy has become a driving socio-economic force, and that digital technology has brought us closer to real time satisfaction of our demands. But if we apply Peck's first tool, we are going to have to discipline ourselves to order our lives more carefully. "Delaying gratification is a process of scheduling the pain and pleasure of life in such a way as to enhance the pleasure by meeting and experiencing the pain first and getting it over with. It is the only decent way to live".

Life teaches us that problems, generally, do not go away when ignored. Best to

---

[113] Arrow

do that homework first, then watch television. Anyone at work who has conquered first in the day the task they least wanted to do, knows that the rest of hours are usually a breeze. Adolescents gradually realise this. Failure to accept it traps people in a cycle of avoidance.

The siren call of a thousand channels of entertainment, millions of web sites, e-mail that may be waiting, a phone call that could be made, the text that might arrive: all this seductive potential can only be handled in an adult manner by understanding where and when to prioritise it and applying some rules rigorously. Microsoft ran a global ad.campaign that promised users infinite possibilities by asking "where do you want to go today?". Often, the answer needs to be "nowhere thanks – here is good and I have some things to do". Web design critic Jakob Nielsen has called the web a "procrastination apparatus". Writing about what he has called "information pollution",[114] he observes that "it can absorb as much time as is required to ensure that you won't get any real work done."

Charles Handy writes of discipline too: he calls it variously "the doctrine of enough", "decent sufficiency" or "a theory of limits". Only personal growth "has no limits. Everything else does". Practically how can we defer gratification and limit ourselves?

The first step is to accept responsibility for what we do. It is not the fault of technology that we are distracted, but the way we use it. Some ideas for discipline include:

- Turn the phone off frequently – don't expect the device to know you need some quiet time.[115]
- Check and respond to e-mail once a day.
- Go for a week every month without watching television. Learn backgammon instead.
- Defer buying new technology until you have wanted it for a year.
- Think twice before you send an e-mail, or cc other people.
- Don't reply to everything.
- Switch off alerts such as sms alerts: it can probably wait until later.
- Block mail totally while you are away: ask people to send it again when you are back if it is important.
- Switch off Instant Messenger unless you are doing only that.

Talking to people, it is clear that many have already evolved their own variants of these – but not in all areas of life. A big problem is the blurring of work and home

---

[114] On his site www.useit.com
[115] Nor the phone operator either – unless they can find a way to charge for this too

Mark Curtis

that we have explored already. If we can work at home because technology permits it, how do we ensure that work does not subtly distract us from family at precisely the time we should be focussing on partners, children or even ourselves? The reverse is also true (Henley Centre call it "homing from work"). Again, new habits of discipline are required. Socially the importance of this cannot be overstated. Peck believes that an inability to delay gratification is transmitted from parents to children: giving time to our children is the way we give them love and that "good discipline requires time". It gives children the feelings of value and self worth which are a framework within which an adult can confidently tackle problems and take responsibility for themselves and their actions. But "almost all of us from time to time seek to avoid – in ways that can be quite subtle – the pain of assuming responsibility for our own problems". A central thesis of this book is that new technology has changed the pattern of our lives so rapidly that we must now tackle the issues thrown up by it as they acquire clarity.

At a social level there are some signs this is recognised. Good examples include the provision of "quiet spaces" in British train carriages, and a ban on the (manual) use of mobile phones in cars – a classic example of technology use with dangerous distraction consequences. Yet it is hard to be confident such legislation will be entirely successful until the vast majority will it to be. In London you do not have to look very hard to see people ignoring the car/phone prohibition. Like drink/driving, it may take a generation or more for values to become socially inculcated. Dealing with distraction technology is a long term challenge. Peck tells a story of how he learnt that he could solve mechanical problems by the simple discipline of taking time to do so. So too, we need to take the time to step back and observe ourselves and think about our technology usage.

Creating space

There is a long and illustrious history of writers, philosophers and divines who recommend the importance to our spiritual and emotional well being of taking time out. Many words describe the process – among them are contemplation, deep thought, introversion, meditation, reflection, rumination, self-examination, self-observation, self-questioning, soul-searching – even prayer. As Charles Handy says "to be quiet and still somewhere, each day, as a discipline, purges the mind".

The surge of interest in Eastern philosophy and religion since the 1960s is a social response to the complexity of modern life, and shows no sign of abating. Classes and courses in Tai Chi, Yoga, Feng Shui, Buddhism and many more are flourishing. In fact a central theme of oriental philosophy has influenced our very thinking on networks – that everything ultimately is connected and interdependent, is a core Buddhist belief.

However an emphasis on space, solitude and quiet has heritage in the European and Judao-Christian tradition too. The Hermits of early Christianity such as St Anthony and Simeon the Stylite (who sat on a pole) led the way. Monasteries institutionalised the idea. Wordsworth romanticised it. British landscape designers of the 18th century placed grottos and follys in country estates to facilitate reflection, in nature. Retreats are a modern re-working of the same notion that time spent alone in silent contemplation can be of immense value. Vipassana meditation courses insist on ten days of silence from pupils. Of the latter I've heard tales of tears and massive mental discomfort, followed by extraordinary spiritual growth. But perhaps we do not need to go to such monkish lengths.

A good start could be to unplug the earphones and listen to the birds sing. To leave the videocamera at home and record everything direct to your brain. To be silent for 10 minutes a day, to take a break from being always on. In their paper "Mobile Email", Japanese researchers Mizuko Ito and Daisuke Okabe use the ghastly term "communications voids" which are "gaps in the day where one is not making interpersonal contact with others…". The spread of the network means that even at the top of a mountain we *can* fill the void. It does not mean that we should.

We could also create social space free from distraction. Looking at this problem my colleagues and I developed a concept we called the *"Focus Bubble"*. It was a response to the fact that etiquette (especially in the business context) has not kept pace with change. As we have seen in many cases it has become harder not easier to hold focussed meetings, and attention spans are declining. In business this affects productivity by reducing the efficiency of face to face encounters. At home it disrupts the time we have for each other.

The Focus Bubble

The Focus Bubble is a technology that makes meetings much more efficient by both diverting outside interruptions and providing tools for better interaction between participants.

Curiously, while technology is clearly disruptive during physical meetings, it is currently extremely poor at enabling good meetings: enhancing enjoyment, interaction and productivity during physical encounters. Also, while there are many good technology tools for individual use, there are few tools that cater well for group interaction. There is a business opportunity here.

The Focus Bubble is a tool which recognises these trends and uses technology to augment meetings with better "across the table" interaction. It could be used at schools and at home too.

Here is how we see it working…

Shortly after Lisa walks into the room where the first project meeting for her company's new food product is held, an alert on her phone asks her if she wants to join the Focus Bubble. This is now accepted practise, and not participating would be a negative statement. The Bubble helps the group to stay focussed and reach decisions, so of course she'll join. She clicks "Yes", and her phone switches into Bubble mode.

Lisa arrived a bit late to the meeting, and she hasn't prepared very well. But she knows that the Focus Bubble will allow her to catch up quickly. On her phone she can get a list of the people invited, the people currently in the Bubble, she can quickly check the agenda, and she can see if any voting has been held yet. The screen also displays the time left for the meeting, and time left for this section of it.

During the first part of the meeting Lisa is pretty inactive, and simply takes things in. Before the first break they all vote on the first issue: support of the new product concept. Lisa votes in favour (anonymously), but she's surprised to see that 2 out of the 5 people in the meeting are actually against it. Without the Bubble, this split of opinion would probably not have emerged until much later, especially since everyone knows that this is the new pet product of the CEO.

At the end of the first session, the Bubble is paused, and Lisa can deal with the two messages that she's received during the meeting: she replies to an SMS from a colleague, and she calls her husband to let him know that she's already bought a birthday present for the girl that they're seeing tonight. They're chatting away on the phone, but when the pause has lasted for 5 minutes, Lisa gets an alert: Bubble re-starts in 30 seconds. She blows a kiss to her husband and gets ready for the next part of the meeting.

The meeting is effective and results-oriented, and the group actually manages to finish 10 minutes early – an unusual luxury. This is partly because the Bubble helped them conduct the meeting uninterrupted, and because it helped the host focus and drive the group towards decisions. Functionality like voting and comment flags was used frequently.

After the Bubble has ended, an alert asks Lisa whether she wants to save the contact details for other participants who she doesn't already have the details for. Of course she will, and she also saves the Bubble itself to her address book, allowing her to simultaneously contact all in the project group when needed.

Lisa's standard Bubble preferences define MMS as the way to deliver any meeting notes, action points, and future agendas to her. Everything that can't be efficiently distributed with that format (multiple photos, bigger audio files, etc.) she can find on the Web using the Bubble URL.[116]

---

[116] The technical solution for a Focus Bubble is principally software operated by standard mobile phones over a BlueTooth network. It could also be enhanced (in a deluxe version) with a separate device that sits in the middle of the meeting space, providing focus (agenda, time left, etc.) and public feedback (voting results, requests to move on, with appropriate sound and visual info, etc.). For set-up at least one phone would need to have the software installed, or download it from a WAP site. The software could then be sent to, or retrieved by, other participants using BlueTooth. One device would act as "host", others would be designated as "guests". In effect the host device is likely to be in the hands of the meeting facilitator. The host would set the parameters of the meeting.

An essential feature of the Bubble is that it blocks out incoming calls and messages on the participants' mobile devices. The Focus Bubble activates such a block for the duration of the meeting: voice messages and text messages are still delivered to recipient's phones, but alerts only show during bubble pauses and after the end of a bubble. A special answer message tells voice callers that the device owner is in a focus meeting, and likewise the user could choose to automatically have SMS responses sent out to incoming messages, signalling the same.

The block remains active for the duration of the meeting or until it is turned off by the user, or when a device moves out of BlueTooth range (this ensures that if a guest leaves in a hurry their device will not remain blocked).

At set-up all guests are registered, and participants who don't have each other's details on their phones automatically exchange digital business cards (a prompt to save them is delayed until after the bubble has ended). The host can choose to publish an agenda, and can set the overall timing of the meeting plus, if required, of individual sections. Focus Bubble will insistently signal the beginning and end of sections and/or the meeting. It will also recommend sections of no longer than 1/2 hour with 5 minute intervals to refocus.

A key role for the focus bubble is to allow participants to signal feelings or feedback that are appropriate but can be hard to communicate or (for the others there) to gauge.

A simple example of this is that guests can use the green (go)/red (end) buttons on their phones to vote for or against an idea or decision. They can also use the up/down arrows on their device to signal degrees of acceptance towards the idea, or overall comfort with the progress of the meeting etc… A colour chart could reveal the aggregated input: red for stop, green for go, amber for neutral etc…

The host will be able to set the meaning of the feedback.

Another useful tool would be the "talking stick" – a rotating permission to speak (perhaps lasting for a limited and equal amount of time for each person) which seeks to ensure all present have a voice, and express their views. The permission would be signalled on the devices or through the central display device.

A "challenge" button (probably limited to one challenge per guest) can at any stage be used to signal real concerns about direction that a guest feels the need to signal. Also, users can send anonymous signals to other participants, for example telling them that they are being disruptive.

Focus Bubble can also play a role in facilitating the recording of a meeting (useful for follow-up, referral and possibly legal reasons too). It could

- record the spoken word of the meeting (if a separate device), plus augmented interactive feedback
- take photographs (if a camera phone) of meeting notes on a whiteboard
- create a web site for these assets
- send selected assets (or links to the website) to participants on the medium of

Mark Curtis

their choice (e-mail, SMS etc..)
- provide a next steps reminder on the medium of their choice (e-mail, automatic calendar entry, SMS etc..)

I'm forever blowing bubbles

Initially, the most obvious use is in business. However, once Focus Bubble is an accepted tool in the business world, there are many ways in which it can be extended to other markets:

- The **Social Bubble** allows me to have a peaceful drink in the pub with my friends, or an uninterrupted dinner with my girlfriend. In this mode, the device used will also enhance the physical experience, but in different ways from in the business meeting.
- The **Personal Bubble** allows me to focus on a task at hand: either solving a problem or meeting a deadline at work. Or it can be used when I need some thinking space. In this mode, the Bubble can help me find creative solutions, it can suggest breaks and stretches, etc.
- The **School Bubble** will be used in classrooms and during further studies. It can significantly enhance group work activities, and allow people to stay in touch. It might even allow teachers to conduct simple tests. In schools that are increasingly classless, the School Bubble will also facilitate bonding in new and more flexible ways.

I've outlined how we need to take personal responsibility for being more disciplined in our use of communications. The bubble is a complementary response that seeks to use communications technology imaginatively to help solve the distraction problem it creates. Many people with teenage children will empathise with the issue. In my family we have striven to find our own ways to create space bubbles, with mixed success. An absolute rule has become to turn off mobiles during meals. At least one social experience then becomes sacrosanct space for face to face conversation (and of course eating). Holidays abroad also create a sort of bubble – partly because mobile contact is so much more expensive and my daughters who are keenly price sensitive, leave their phones at home. We all notice the benefit of better, deeper interaction between us.

Disengagement is hard. Part of the trick is to free ourselves from the tyranny of time. Ever since medieval monasteries fixed duties and ritual to each minute of the day, we have gradually increased our slavery to time – most of all when factory owners began to insist on punctuality – a word which did not come into use until the 1770's. Nineteenth century French towns and villages set great store by their church bells – even in an age of rampant anti-clericalism these literally told the time to workers in the field and workshop alike, and the bells were symbols of civic pride.[117] Theodore Zeldin in "An Intimate History of Humanity"[118] points to research which has found that two thirds of French people "suffered tensions in their relationships with time, and that the well-educated and the rich were the most dissatisfied of all. The wider the choices before them, and the more numerous their desires, the less time they have to give to each one…Technology has been a rapid heartbeat, compressing housework, travel, entertainment, squeezing more and more into the allotted span. Nobody expected that it would create the feeling that life moves too fast".

In that classic of the self-help/business genre, the "Seven Habits of Effective People"[119], Steven Covey outlines a number of ways in which humans can achieve more of their personal goals. One of the seven habits is the "principle of balanced self renewal".[120] He also calls it taking time to "sharpen the saw" as opposed to relentlessly using it. The concept is simple: it is good for us to spend time doing a wide variety of things that improve our physical health, heighten our emotional awareness and spread our spiritual wings. He also fingers TV as the greatest obstacle to this. Yet the media picture is now much more complex than when he wrote. Taking "time out" from being always on is when we can sharpen our saws. Personally I like to immerse myself in the natural world, or buy and cook food, or go for long vigorous cycle rides. All of these renew me. Increasingly I find that I need to ensure the digital environment – via a mobile phone – does not come with me. No-one should imagine this is easy: there is always an excuse. For example on a100 mile ride a phone gives me the ability to call and ask for help in the event that something unfixable goes wrong with the bike. It can carry a map too. But I've found that when I have it with me in a back pocket I still feel, in some hard to define way, moored to a different context. The potential for it to ring is always there. Without it I am free to float mentally on my wheels. I am convinced we need to learn how to cut loose to really renew our edge.

The Open Corporation

What is true for individuals is also true for organisations. Digital communications have changed the way in which companies (and other institutions) operate, often in unexpected ways. One long term effect will be to split them wide open to greater

---

[117] See Village Bells by Alain Corbin
[118] Minerva
[119] Simon & Schuster
[120] Not dissimilar to Scott Peck's fourth tool of Discipline – "Balancing"

Mark Curtis

scrutiny. Possibly we are seeing the dawn of the open organisation. We have seen that privacy is going to be increasingly rare for individuals. Why should it be different for commerce, government or charities? It will not be, and there are four reasons why – everything is recorded, the system is porous, public expectations have changed and openness will confer competitive advantage for the first to embrace it.

All the big scandals that engulfed (largely US based) corporations in 2002 had a common factor beyond wrong-doing: e-mail audit trails. USA Today reported in January 2002: "the job of recovering the missing Enron accounting documents is falling to computer sleuths whose work can foil the casual use of the delete button. They've been called on before in high-profile cases, looking for suspected spy transmissions and missing Clinton White House e-mails. And now they'll be asked to recover documents from the computers of Arthur Andersen, which acknowledges its employees destroyed thousands of e-mails and paper documents about Enron. Investigators want to know who knew about the problems at Enron, which shocked the financial world and its own employees with its fall from Wall Street grace to bankruptcy." The ghost in the machine is a history of communication. The obsession with accurate back-ups in case crucial data is lost, has an unintended side effect. Records are kept of transactions that fraudsters would prefer to have disappeared for ever. The lesson is that you can delete all you like from your local machine, but the network still knows what you've been up to.

That is one way in which it becomes harder for companies to keep secrets: much of their communication is systematically recorded. The second way is that their walls are irretrievably leaky. E-mail has become a prime tool for discussing issues internally, but also makes it so easy for whistleblowers to despatch inside information to the outside world. They do this either directly from their desktop PC, or on digital or even printed copies, smuggled out of the office. The UK government seems to suffer especially from this – remember the infamous Jo Moore e-mail suggesting the government use September 11th as a good day to "bury" bad news. The terrible photographs from Iraq's Abu Ghraib prison reinforce the point: distributed by mobile phone and Internet they told a graphic tale many in the US military hierarchy would have liked to suppress. No wonder so many companies have moved to ban camera phones, though they are surely whistling in the wind.

The third reason why openness is the agenda, is a corollary of the above point: because digital *can* open up the guts of an organisation to public gaze, we *will* increasingly expect it to. These days most companies have a web site. Many use extranets – web sites where selected partners or customers can interact with them but only on presentation of a password. Intranets too are popular; these are basically internal web sites, used as tools for management and communication. On a typical Intranet one might expect to see internal jobs advertised, directories of e-mail addresses and telephone numbers, latest news, meeting room booking tools, shared documents. Some of this content may also be published to extranets, and even the public facing web site. It is only levels of network and security that seem to determine the difference between whether information is kept private or let loose. But theoretically we know that the IP based technology permits easy communication flows between layers. The walls are permeable, and that potential is increasingly understood by stakeholders. Once again (in this book) *potential* is a key word. Reasonable reflection tells us that it is hard to walk into a building and insist on seeing information stuck inside a filing cabinet or lurking in an in-tray (if you know where it is anyway). The potential to find out what you want to know is less in the pre-digital world because it is just so much harder. Post-digital that is all changing. The organisations that understand and act on this may be able to build some clear differentiation for themselves too.

So the fourth driver along the road to the open organisation will ironically be the usual engines of capitalism. The quest for edge will lead institutions to consider carefully how open they could be. Real time reporting systems are giving companies daily information about their performance. As noted earlier in this book, results are now routinely released to the stock market not at annual, but at quarterly intervals. Updates and warnings come in between. At some stage more adventurous corporations might seek to stand out from the crowd, by keeping their shareholders and customers informed about performance, with little or no delay between the internal collation of data and its public release. If the "fat cats" desire their bonuses, perhaps we could insist on this provision of more immediate information as a quid pro quo.

Grace Under Pressure

There are other ways in which we can expect change in corporate behaviour. Mastering the art of digital listening would be a good start for all kinds of organisations. By this I mean the ability to handle incoming communication with grace. More than once I've discussed their public web sites with well known companies, and been surprised to hear that they either wished to discourage communication from customers or at best did not know what to do with it (in which case they defaulted to avoidance tactics). Do they not wish to talk with their customers? Often the answer is only "to" and not "with". This attitude cannot survive digital.

Ursula Hews[121] captures the frustration of modern customer relations well: "Let us say that a customer has been delivered the wrong product and rings up to the customer service department of a company to complain. Having dutifully worked

---

[121] The Making of a Cybertariat. (Merlin). Though her example is a phone call, the story is typical of all kinds of communication. Also, the operator will be using digital technology to structure their (inadequate) response, and it could be applied much more effectively.

Mark Curtis

her way through a series of menus and pressed the required keys she has been placed in a queue where, between bursts of recorded music, she is informed "Your call is valuable to us. Please hold"...when she finally reaches the front of the line, instead of being able to give vent to...justified annoyance, she is immediately cut off with a series of scripted requests for information. What is her address and zip code? What is her order reference number?...Could she confirm her name?...Any slight deviation from the norm...puts her into a special category that requires being put into another queue...Both worker and customer are trapped in a situation beyond either's control, and unpleasant for both. Instead of embarking on a joint effort to solve the problem, they are pitted against each other...and the pressure on the service worker to meet productivity targets forbids the kind of social chat that can transform a chore into a pleasure when people meet..."

Hews' vignette implicitly points at a whole number of solutions to the problem of better corporate listening. They include:

- Structure e-mail and call help systems so that each customer has a case worker who sticks with them
- To back this up, make information available cross department
- Use language which creates co-operation from the off ("Hello. What is the problem we are going to solve?")
- Respond to e-mails rapidly and with a restatement of the client's issue
- Organise call centre staff in teams where they share problems and solutions with each other
- Give those teams a name so the customer (and the staff) has something to hang onto ("it'll be me and the Banana team helping you sort this – always ask for us when you call..")
- Show photos of the teams on the web site (it makes it more personal)
- Report each team's satisfaction targets on the web site!
- Recognise that time is something customers will pay to use as they choose: offer premium services which give higher standards of service
- Create a one number standard[122]
- Call customers back
- Give staff a direct number for customers
- Make "how to contact us" very clear on the web site and offer customers a number of alternatives
- Answer standard questions on the web site

---

[122] As I write this I have had to call five different numbers in one day (starting with a helpful looking "any questions" number I found on a web site) to resolve a simple question about my car lease agreement. I still have to call back tomorrow, because the final number called was a department which had closed for the day.

Cost conscious finance directors may regard the above list with considerable suspicion. I contend that there are big benefits for those who understand that new standards of customer care are required in the digital era. These include lower staff turnover rates because they'll like the work more. In the US and the UK 90% of call centre staff leave each year. Other advantages include better knowledge sharing, lower transaction costs with customers (trust goes up), and greater coherence of organisational action (the left hand knows what the right hand is doing). The argument also applies to outbound communication. Those who get it right by adopting a "less is more" approach to promotion, and ensuring that what they do send is highly relevant, will be in for big rewards from time-conscious consumers.

It will probably take some time for this vision to be realised. Few organisations are good at change. Customer relationship management (CRM) has been around for a while, but there is little evidence that most companies are any good at it. Habits are ingrained and it takes a lot of energy to displace them, usually catalysed by some sort of crisis. My argument is that unsustainable levels of communication are just such a crisis. It may be hard, and long, work to shift our corporate behaviour.

Building Cathedrals

Because of our obsession with immediacy – the have it now culture – we are at risk of undervaluing the longer term project in society. Charles Handy points out that when mediaeval stonemasons began work on a cathedral, they knew it was unlikely that they would live to see the building in its entirety. Finding it hard to imagine such a mindset, I wonder if we should re-embrace it? Long term thinking – imagining the effects of what we do way into the future – is one way of ensuring responsible behaviour now. It may also have the happy consequence of creating enduring monuments for humanity of the future to cherish, much as we do the Pyramids, the Great Mosque in Cordoba and Chartres Cathedral. One person who is doing this is inventor Danny Hillis. " Think of the oak beams in the ceiling of College Hall at New College, Oxford. Last century, when the beams needed replacing, carpenters used oak trees that had been planted in 1386 when the dining hall was first built. The 14th-century builder had planted the trees in anticipation of the time, hundreds of years in the future, when the beams would need replacing. Did the carpenters plant new trees to replace the beams again a few hundred years from now?"[123]

Hillis is working on a clock that ticks just once a year and will last for 10,000. He imagines the cuckoo coming out once a millennia, a hand moving every century. Brian Eno has called it the Clock of the Long Now. Hillis recognizes that this may be a covert attempt to immortalize part of himself – but that may not be such an ignoble

---

[123] From an article in Hotwired at http://www.wired.com/wired/scenarios/clock.html

Mark Curtis

desire if the result is a message that he cared about the future enough to act on it.

What Hillis is doing is startling and inspiring because it is so counter to modern trends. Someone recently asked me to explain what is so great about long term thinking. After all, the 1000 year Reich was an infamous example of the elongated view. But all that proves is that we can always pervert a way of looking at life. When I think of some things I value, many have acquired the patina of age, like the buildings above. Even in an age of easy divorce, we esteem the long and happy marriage (knowing too that such things are never easy, we admire the couple for their commitment.) I have an old coat that has seen many mountains, been drenched by dreary Scottish rain and held trout in its pocket. It is falling apart now but I cannot give it up for it is woven with memory. Clothing company Howies distinguish themselves partly by a dedication to making (cool) clothes which last, because that is more sustainable. My favourite modern novel[124] was published in instalments over a period of 25 years, covers 60 in the narrative, and as a result is the single best picture of life in England in the 20th century that I know of. Great musicians practice incessantly and their talent grows. In our family is an old fashioned Roberts radio, inherited from a deceased grandfather. It still works perfectly. Where are the new technology equivalents of Roberts Radios? Perhaps, we could teach long term thinking in school, and nurture personal creativity of the kind Hillis represents at the same time.

Celebrating Ourselves

So far I have suggested that we need to grapple with distraction by building habits of discipline and disengagement, both as individual citizens and as institutions. Belief in the value of the long-term project may help too. The last response is to celebrate our individuality. There are three aspects to this – playing our part, doing so with responsibility, and unleashing our creativity.

When we feel self-worth, we take care of ourselves. Alcoholics and people with eating disorders unfortunately show this to be true; their unhappiness with themselves manifests itself physically. As Scott Peck says "self discipline is self caring". Feeling valuable makes our time valuable. As we have seen, engaging with social networks can really help with this, and the web has afforded endless new opportunities for the shy, the bored, the chatty and the insecure to engage.

As we have seen commentators have observed the rise of "personal authority" as opposed to institutional authority. Willmott and Nelson[125] have shown how, right across Europe, friends and relatives play a greater role in purchase decisions than any other source. This is more marked among the young. We are building our own

---

[124] A Dance to the Music of Time by Anthony Powell
[125] Complicated Lives (Wiley)

networks of influence rather than accepting at face value the word of the government, or the BBC, or school. In touch with millions of viewpoints we can explore
more fully what we believe, and contribute too in a global discourse.

A key part of this is to take responsibility for our actions. We have seen that distance
does not always lend itself to responsible behaviour and I suggest that again a habit of
discipline will come in handy to balance our increased reach and influence. It is easy
to abuse the facility of a forum, or e-mail, to express opinions that are poorly thought
through, offensive, hurtful or damaging. Possibly the most memorable of Covey's Seven
Habits is "seek first to understand, then to be understood". In other words – shut up and
listen with all your senses before you try to get your view across. It is a habit we would
do well to use more often in the digital arena. Razorfish was a passionate collection of
people. When the market for what the company did fell away from beneath its feet, life
got tough. Redundancies began. Management was criticised. At the time there were two
web sites which specialised in a subversive way in rumours about companies – Fucked
Company and The Vault. Both had message boards to which anyone could contribute.
Gradually a large Razorfish discussion group grew on both, much to the discomfort
of "management". Eventually as things became grim, somebody published the CEO's
address and mobile number and encouraged others to hassle him. Other senior people
came in for nasty criticism. Stupidly, access to both sites was then cut off from within
the company network. I say stupid because a) it drew attention to the offending material
and b) everyone looked from home anyway. I thought that we made a mistake when we
blocked access. Perhaps there should have been an internal forum. In retrospect I realise
that the anonymous posters were equally to blame. The company had some big problems, and discussion of these should have been in the open. But ill-informed personal
attacks were, well, irresponsible. I think a good rule here would be that you should never
say anything digitally you are not prepared to say face to face with someone one foot
taller than you. It is a crucial part of any new social contract we evolve that if we undermine corporate authority with personal authority, we do so with a sense of responsibility.
This looks like a lesson that may take time to learn.

Celebrating our individuality therefore does not have to be at odds with the emphasis we have seen on social networks in the previous chapter. We saw how we can and
are using communications technology to build new, closer networks of association, and
that digital media can enhance communities. However this should not be at the expense
of our sense of who we are – and there are signs that in the right hands the new technology can enable an even stronger sense of identity. The right hands are of course those
of the ordinary person as opposed to the owners of media channels. The latter tend to
throw so many images at us that they confuse our identity. Being creative with the new
technology to create "personal content" is another trend now set to explode. If we grasp
the opportunities presented to us to create and build memories, which we alone own, we
can fashion precious uniqueness, yet use it too to relate to other people.

PART TWO
The Social Potential Of New Technology

Chapter Twelve
The rise of personal content

Paul and Heather live in Peckham, South East London. Paul is a project manager for National Construction Week, an annual event which aims to get young people interested in the building trade. He is from Sheffield, and in the past has managed bands, been a radio producer in Seville and a Labour councillor in Chiswick. Heather, his wife, is a civil servant and a vicar's daughter. She has created a web site for Paul. Her skills, which include the animation software Flash, are all self taught. Over time, she just realised she could, and her confidence grew. She is still learning, and has developed clear views on the need for simplicity in web design.

Paul had never touched a computer before1999. The next year his job with the Millennium Commission came to an end. He realised that he did not want to "turn into a 45 year old burnt out bloke, out of touch with the way the world works." He discovered that the domain name www.paulbower.com was still available. He registered it with the initial intention of putting up his CV – "it was a kind of announcement". Go there and you find a simple web site which tells you about Paul's past, present and his plans for the future. Two extra features stand out. Heather has created a Flash doll of Paul in his underpants which visitors can dress from a clothes rail. The joke is perhaps a private one: Paul is obsessed with well cut suits. You can also find a link to Paul's blog. He is an articulate and funny man, with much to say – usually about politics, often about his family. That he cares deeply about both is evident. Having his own site has made a difference. Meeting up with a large group of old friends from the US at a fiesta in Spain, he was delighted to find that several of them knew of his site, and read it. The drummer and bassist from his old punk rock band recently tracked him down: they "googled" him by putting his name in Google. Interviewing for a new job recently he found himself more confident around questions concerning technology – "I have my own web site". He got the position.

Like Paul and Heather, millions of people worldwide have also discovered the wonderful power that digital communication gives them to project themselves. In a host of different ways, they are creating and making available personal content.

Digital technology facilitates this like no other. Pen, printing press, painting, penny post, photography, photocopier; none of these conferred such power on ordinary people to communicate so widely as does the combination of web and mobile technology.

There are examples now all round us – from teenage blogs to soldier's record of conflict despatched almost live from the front line. The most lauded web sites in the world, eBay and Amazon thrive on personal content. The dividing line between the traditional media world of newspapers, TV and radio and personal content is becoming blurred. One consequence is that the former institutions seem a little less remote every day. Another is that we ourselves are becoming the media "product".

In South Korea they've gone one step better: an online newspaper entirely created by personal content is displacing "big" media – Oh My News. Over 90% of its content is supplied by "citizen reporters" who not only get to see their name in print, but also are paid (about $20) per article. Oh My News is so influential that newly elected President Roh Moo-Hyun granted his first interview to it in February 2005. Bold fringe experiment indulged by a politican you may be thinking…Oh My News has 1.2 million readers and has the third biggest circulation in South Korea.[126]

Why is this so important? This chapter, after looking at some examples of personal content, examines four reasons. Firstly it gives people the chance to celebrate their individuality. Secondly we can record and capture memories in new and exciting ways. Related to this is the third reason: the age old human quest for immortality, to leave one's mark on the world. Lastly, personal content implies an act of creation, and there is much fulfilment to be sought in this.

Who is the media owner now?

Ten years ago, one of the ways in which radio stations used to sell themselves to advertisers was by claiming that they were more proximate to their listeners. Figure One shows how this works: in research people tend to place radio stations as closer to them (they might know where the studios are, or perhaps their brother's friend works there) than other media. Additionally the scale of radio makes it not much "bigger than me" – or at least not when compared with say, Hollywood. The world of films is clearly both much bigger than most people (they cost millions to make) and a long way away (I'm unlikely ever to meet Brad Pitt). TV comes next down the scale, with magazines and newspapers somewhere between TV and radio.

---

[126] From Ahonen and Moore: "Communities Dominate Brands" (Futuretext)

Mark Curtis

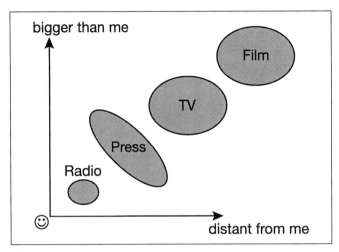

Figure 1

If you buy or sell media space, it's an interesting model. But it has changed. Now factor in the Internet, Mobile, Digital TV and radio.

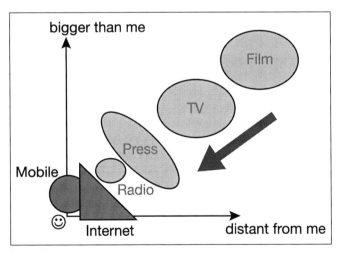

Figure 2

Mobile media are clearly as close to me as you can get: the Finnish for mobile translates as "handy". The Internet is not much further out. One reason for this is personal content. Because I can interact with these new digital media (add stuff, ask questions), and not just act in the role of dumb receiver, they tend to become more intimate.[127] Another reason is that the new media are always on, and do not follow a time-based schedule like a TV channel. This makes them feel more configurable around each person's needs. And the new media can be personalised to deliver exactly what the user wishes. A Google search is an example many will be familiar with.

Partly as a result of the proximity of new media to consumers, the established media are moving inexorably downstream towards us.[128] This is hugely important because the impetus to commercialise our "content" is a trend that is accelerating, enabled and given fresh drive by digital media. We are being encouraged to spend our time publishing, because what we have to say is valuable. The ivory towers set up for example by public broadcasters and national newspapers are being dismantled as more people participate in media content. Examples include:

- Voting on major issues on news web sites. Note that this gives instant feedback, sense of participation and content (the aggregated results) to the news service
- Radio (not just phone ins) now using text as a primary form of audience interaction – BBC's Radio 5 encourages a constant stream of this. It has (almost a brand in its own right) 606, not just a football phone in but also a text service and a discussion forum on the web
- Journalists signing articles with their e-mail address
- The fact that the BBC recently adopted a fourth value – "to connect"
- Amazon publish lists written by customers of their favourite music: useful for recommendations of new stuff to buy (from Amazon of course)
- Betfair bases its business on making a market between ordinary punters who create and sell bets and those who buy them
- P2P services such as Kazaa exist only because users make their content available to each other (though record companies may dispute exactly who owns the content)
- Big Brother takes a handful of average people and lets us observe and overhear them for weeks on end. Their mundane conversations are reported through multiple media. Also the ability of the audience to affect content (e.g.: voting housemates out)

---

[127] This is not always the case: big picture Hollywood web sites are low on real interaction (beyond games), and still tend to convey the impression that they are from a different and altogether bigger planet than most of us. Perhaps that is suitable for their core medium which seeks to enthral and entertain.
[128] Again, probably not including film – yet.

Mark Curtis

Reality TV, as many have noted, is particularly interesting for the way it implies that we are all fascinating enough to be media content.[129] In these programmes the daily and often mundane activities and conversations of participants become news in their own right: which is the content not only for the programme but also for the parasitic tabloids which feed off the former. This points to a further trend: the line between news and entertainment is getting blurred too. Competition in the global news space and the appetite of newspapers for celebrity stories has partly driven this. Digital takes it further. Media content – including that which I make – is now potentially both entertainment and news for the people I share it with. We can see this clearly with blogs.

So – "big" media is moving closer to us, and we are getting closer to it because we publish our own stuff much more easily. In fact we become embedded – part of the product itself. What then are leading examples of this personal content?

The easiest to spot are forums and chat zones. We've looked at these extensively in the context of social networks and digital communications. The importance of community to the Internet is well known, and personal content is the raw material on which an industry has been built. These are places where views are exchanged, contact made, help proffered. The model is dialogue, the start point conversation.

A growing type of personal content is recommendations. Amazon has used this brilliantly. Customers can record their views on books, music and other items through reviews, ratings and lists of favourites. Other customers can even rate the ratings to make the service more useful and trustworthy. This may not strike some observers as personal content: in my view, when it involves an act of creation, it unequivocally is. This definition might rule out rating, but must surely include a 200 word review or imaginative list of favourite albums for late night listening. The user is putting a little bit of themselves on-line, not only for others to enjoy but also to meet some inner needs.

Viewed like this, the question of ownership begins to darken the doorway. Who owns my carefully crafted review on Amazon – me or them? Does that matter to me? Arguably in this example, it matters very little to me and a great deal to Amazon who need to be very sure of themselves on issues of Intellectual Property (IP). The community side of the Internet has grown so spectacularly because ordinary people are not even remotely concerned with IP. This may change.

Many people who use the Apple iPod and its associated software, iTunes, have discovered the usefulness and pleasure to be gained from ratings and playlists. In essence, these allow you to rate any or all songs in your digital collection from one

---

[129] Though this trend may be reaching the end of its life: reality TV shows seem now to be ditching "ordinary' (read dull) people in exchange for either celebrities or participants with obvious extremes of personality. Or both if they can be happily combined!

to five stars, and to create playlists for any occasion. These may be for running, for the Friday night party, for a long car trip, for a wedding – it's all up to the user. We can all be DJ's this way. We can also share our output with others. If your iTunes computer is on a network it will detect other iTunes enabled machines and let you (with their owner's permission) listen to their playlists. Sounds too techy? I know of teenagers who take their iPods to parties and compete over who gets to play their list. Sounds too teenage? A forty-something acquaintance of mine recently went on a long car journey. He'd never seen an iPod before. The owner of the car he was travelling in used an FM adaptor to play it through the radio. Then the car behind tuned in to the same frequency and they shared music on the motorway. They had become a radio station. How can the music business police *that*?

The music industry is quite clear: IP in the music you and I buy, whether in a shop or as a download, remains with them. But who owns the playlist that turns you into a popular radio station among your friends and colleagues? For most people, unfamiliar with the legal niceties, the difference is hard to distinguish. The music I carry around with me feels like mine, especially when I've gone to lots of bother to rate and order it. The boundaries between someone else's content and mine become very blurred.

Personal digital content of a different kind has also developed legal ramifications in another, more deadly arena. In 1914, when the First World War broke out, my grandfather was working on a farm in Africa. He sold the only thing of value he owned, his saddle, and bought a ticket back to England with the proceeds. Once returned he joined up. He saw action at Ypres and on the Somme, where in October 1916 he took a bullet through the leg while leading a grenade attack on a German trench. After spending 18 hours in a watery shell hole, he was rescued by stretcher bearers. It was too late however to save the leg, which was amputated in a field hospital. Back in Manchester, he lay fighting for life in a hospital ward, unable to see the end of the room for the smog that drifted in through the open windows. He was decorated with the Military Cross, though he never would say why. He was 97 when he died, living in a small terraced house in Majorca.

Although as a small boy I quizzed him incessantly, I know much of the detail of this because he left behind him a typed manuscript of his wartime experiences, some photos, and his medals. The pictures show nothing graphic or shocking. They are of friends. A handsome and smiling man in uniform is noted on the reverse as 2nd Lt Macdonald of his regiment. A few years ago I found Macdonald's name carved in marble. It was on the side of Lutyen's famous Thiepval memorial to the many thousands missing (and never found) on the Somme battlefield. It was a sombre moment, a stony black and white exposure to the past. Somewhere in France my grandfather had pressed the shutter that glimpsed his friend on film for a fraction of a second. Months later he had been erased in all but memory.

Mark Curtis

Ninety years later, American soldiers in Iraq have also been busy creating personal content. Unlike my ancestor's mementoes, their work is graphic, has been made available for all to see, and close to the time that they captured it in Abu Ghraib jail. Susan Sontag, a historian of photography, has written about this in the Guardian[130] newspaper. For her the photos "reflect a shift in the use made of pictures – less objects to be saved than evanescent messages to be disseminated, circulated. A digital camera is a common possession of most soldiers. Where once photographing war was the province of photojournalists, now the soldiers themselves are all photographers – recording their war, their fun, their observations of what they find picturesque, their atrocities – and swapping images among themselves, and emailing them around the globe." Political commentator Andrew Marr, writing in the Daily Telegraph makes a similar observation. "…Now we have the Nokia Aftermath[131] – a zone of conflict whose prisons and darker corners can be captured with tiny digital cameras, or even mobile phones, and then instantly sent around the world". As he points out, this may be for the better, as it closes the gap between what the soldier and the citizen at home knows. I share his feeling that it is doubtful the First World War would have made it much beyond 1915 if this technology had been available. Public support would have been fatally undermined by pictures of the horror.

This is therefore a positive message to come out of a sorry tale. We have to hope that those people in power who wish to ban the creation of personal content in controversial situations are defeated by the sheer ubiquity of the means to do it. This is the power of the new technology: to reach into corners of our lives and allow us to shine lights into the darkness, to reorder our priorities and create new opportunities for ourselves by doing so.

Neil and Ben live with their baby, Minnie, in Wiltshire. Ben is Danish, immaculate, thoughtful and kind. She is thinking about what next to do in her career. Neil is a revolutionary by nature – always mentally on the move and challenging the status quo. Their house is tidy, uncluttered. During a time not so long ago when incomes were uncertain, they experimented with selling unwanted possessions on eBay. A sweep through the house revealed mobile phone chargers, bits of old computer, books, Cd's, furniture – all of which they could live happily without. To their amazement the first sale brought in £1700. Now they refer ironically to everything they own as 'stock', and repeat the exercise from time to time. It's a sort of profitable digital spring clean. This may not be an approach to life everyone could stomach: but all Neil and Ben have done, it seems to me, has been to realise that there was another kind of personal content they could trade.

In their case, this is not so surprising, as Neil had already used the power of

---

[130] 25 May 2004.
[131] 12 May 2004. Nokia now sell more cameras (embedded in phones) than any other camera brand.

the Internet to reinvent himself. Having made the decision to promote the idea of what he calls 'Authentic Business', he wrote an e-mail to 4000 people announcing what he intended to do, and invited them to participate. The core was to be a regular e-mail newsletter with contributions from like-minded people who Neil began to discover, through his network. A web site[132] followed shortly after. Then a book. Now he runs a thriving business helping companies which are concerned with more than just the profit motive, to be true to their values.

It is not necessary to turn one's personal content into a business to get enjoyment from it. Fans create web pages celebrating every kind of entertainment, where you can frequently learn more than on "official" sites. Even products are speculatively evolved by individuals: at one site you can see over a hundred ideas for the iPod of the future submitted by enthusiastic amateurs.[133]

Most accessible of all, the blogging movement is the fastest growing sector of the web, currently its most interesting, and is set to exploit a wider potential by going mobile too. In April 2005, according to Technorati[134], 38,000 new blogs are being created and half a million new entries being made every day. As mentioned earlier, a blog is a form of web based journal. There are some distinct characteristics most have. Firstly they are time based, which gives a structure for content most readers can understand with ease. It also encourages regular submissions by the author. Secondly most blogs invite commentary from visitors. This can develop into lively debate – in some cases tantamount to a community hosted and given energy by the owner. Other popular features include the ability to post pictures, archive, link to elsewhere and show lists (for instance of favourite current movies). In Japan it is polite to use 'trackback', which in effect leaves the digital equivalent of a calling card ("I've made a comment about your blog on my blog and thought you might like to know").

Is Paul, who we met earlier, a typical blogger with his mixture of personal experience and political observation? You might expect so – after all in the early years of the Internet, the majority of users were men. But blogging is at least as much female as male. A leading blog service is Livejournal[135]. Today they have over 6.5 million accounts. 1.5 million of these have been updated in the last 30 days, 338,000 in the last 24 hours. 67% of their users are female. Only half of their bloggers reside in the US. More than 16,000 are from the Ukraine. There are 180,000 in the UK – that is four well attended premiership football games! The highest percentage of users are aged 18. The bulk are between 14 and 26. Indeed almost four times more us-

---

[132] www.authenticbusiness.com
[133] http://gallery.ipodlounge.com/ipod
[134] www.technorati.com
[135] www.livejournal.com

Mark Curtis

ers are 14 than 28. According to a survey by MIT[136], 55% of bloggers provide their real names. These figures may come as a surprise to those who don't know what blogging is, still think the Internet is an irrelevance, or that only spotty young men and paedophiles make use of it. Imagine what happens as this generation of women hits their twenties and begin to use blogging as an everyday tool of life. It may be another five years – but it will go mainstream.

The content of blogs is of course mixed. It can be inspired, mundane, insightful and elitist in equal doses. Some are appallingly self referential and smug. But what I might think is irrelevant: they matter to the people who publish them and those in their social network who consume and add to them.. Just as no-one in their right mind would find all conversations in the world equally stimulating, so each blog presumably fulfils a role, or if not will wither and die. Not everyone's story will be interesting. However blog readership jumped 58% in 2004 and is now 27% of Internet users.[137]

The next development in personal publishing is mobile. Already the uncomfortable word moblogging has been pressed into service to describe the ability to publish to a web site journal direct from your phone. Nokia has launched a new product called Lifeblog. This is software, on your phone and PC, which keeps a record of your life as automatically as possible, and arranges it for you in a timeline, or diary format. Currently it not only captures the photos and videos you take with your phone, it also keeps all the SMS (texts) and MMS that you send and receive. This may not sound very useful to some: but ask teenage girls in many countries what they most fear about losing their phones. It is not the address list, even though rebuilding that can be lengthy and painful. It is the loss of sentimental and meaningful texts and photos that cannot be stored elsewhere that they worry about. Watch groups of young people in public places passing phones from hand to hand, to compare pictures and funny texts. Once again content becomes a way of defining self. Great care is taken to give names to pictures, which add to the story telling.

For Lifeblog the next step has been for the software to offer sharing of personal content over the web, which since late 2004 it has been able to do. As predicted by Ursula Hews, something social, which is currently done for free, will take on a commercial angle if people are willing to pay for such a service. I think they will because this creation and sharing of personal content is compelling. Why?

The most obvious reason is that through this we project our sense of self, both to ourselves and others. I am convinced that 50% of the intended audience for any one blog is the author. Heather and Paul are sharing a public joke about Paul's addiction

---

[136] http://web.media.mit.edu/~fviegas/survey/blog/results

[137] Pew /Internet January 2005. They also report that 62% of online Americans do not know what blogs are – which is why I am not assuming that readers of Distraction will either.

to suits. Molly tells us lots about her love of music.[138] Christian gets emotional about design and food.[139] As Susan Greenfield says, the most precious thing we have is our private ego, so under threat in the modern world. What we need more than ever is "celebration of individuality". The paradox is that by sharing this, we both proclaim ourselves to be who we are, and participate in the network too by feeding it content and creating links. If the network is the future, personal content can prevent it from eliminating our identities.

The second motivation for personal content creation is to render up memories for the future. This is the "digital shoebox"[140], but not one kept in the attic with few notes or explanation. Imagine much of your daily doings captured for review at a later date. Sounds improbable? This is definitely where Lifeblog is tentatively stepping. Remember your phone knows where you are, who you have talked to and is capable of recording (for a while at least) all your conversations. What kind of record of family history might be revealed in this way? Greenfield imagines a future where we can access our past, almost as it was, because it has all been recorded as it happened, and can be digitally re-created.[141] Such a vision is still some way off, but we should consider the impact of increased digital memories now. Until the mid nineteenth century very few except the rich had any real idea of family history stretching back over more than three generations. For the wealthy, painting formed an exclusive (and expensive) visual record of the past they had inherited. Photography gave the masses a better sense of where they had come from. It put people in touch with history, brought long dead relatives and their environment closer. Tatty old pictures can reveal much in the detail – the lines etched on faces that worked hard, the clothes worn each day, a dog in the foreground, children playing in the background. Now with digital cameras, phones, PC's, blogs etc..we are creating, capturing and creating at a furious rate compared with the past. Historians in the future will have their work cut out assessing source material: there will just be so much of it.

For we are leaving digital traces of ourselves everywhere we go, like snails winding across a garden on a summer's night. It is, in a small way, another step on mankind's path of ambition, which reaches ultimately towards immortality. Does a blog of my life make any difference? Will anyone look when I am dead? Probably few: but I'd like to think my children will, and theirs too, and maybe beyond. History is the collective memory of society; without it we would be prisoners of the now,

---

[138] www.socialbeasts.com

[139] www.christianlindholm.com

[140] see blog above on this

[141] Without mental context though: as she points out, you may be able to see the sunset on a beach you experienced but you'll still have to remember what you felt.

condemned to relearn each and every lesson of humanity in an endless and un-productive cycle. I know a little about some of my ancestors: way back there is a Huguenot strain. I would love to know more of this: did they flee France after the Revocation of the Edict of Nantes in the 1680's? Where did they settle? What was their trade? What did they think? Is data all most of us are destined to leave? Perhaps. Yet to provide answers for future generations is a powerful outcome of any deep need I may have to leave my mark on this world.

In fact the significance may lie in the act of creation itself. Ecologist Stefan Harding of Schumaker College says that the two positive things mankind is best at are art and celebration. Twenty years ago I visited a remarkable place where creativity had changed people's lives. Barlinnie Jail is the last surviving Victorian prison in Glasgow. It is a grim granite fortress, squatting toadlike in the East End. Currently it is home to the only man convicted of the Lockerbie bombing. From the 1970's until it was closed in 1993, the Bar-L as it is known locally, was home to the Special Unit, an extraordinary experiment in custodial policy. It was set up as a last gasp answer to the problem of recidivist prisoners: those who seemingly could not give up violence and trouble making once inside jail. Its most famous inmate was Jimmy Boyle, once dubbed the most violent man in Scotland by the tabloids. In his book, "A Sense of Freedom" Boyle described the Unit. Prisoners accustomed to brutal behaviour and treatment found themselves in an environment where they were allowed to wear their own clothes, watch television and other privileges. If they wanted something, the staff would vote on whether it could be allowed, which encouraged the inmates to lobby and reason for what they wanted, not fight. More remarkably they were encouraged to explore the creative side of themselves through writing, music and art. There was a memorable moment when Boyle realised that they were to be allowed the use of scissors – unthinkably dangerous in the environment of confinement and violence he had come from.

After a phase of bewilderment at this new level of trust and responsibility, Boyle settled in, and eventually began to write and create some astonishing art. One piece showed an attenuated figure lying among bars which pushed vertically up through every angle of his limbs and around his prostate body. It clearly communicated how in prison, the bars are not just arranged around you, but go through you too. Other prisoners such as Hugh Collins, also benefited hugely from the Special Unit, which remained controversial throughout its history. Boyle was eventually released, got married, and set up a drug rehabilitation unit for young people in Edinburgh, where he still lives. Collins is a novelist living in Edinburgh.

The Special Unit had a clear message:[142] when the energy that runs through us all is channelled into creative outlets, it can be very powerful. Digital technology

---

[142] To be clear: not all prisoners could cope with it and a few asked to go back to the traditional system.

gives us the opportunity and the tools. We might simply take photos and organise and edit them. We might publish our thoughts and lives on-line. We might share our passions for music and books and art by making lists and recommending enjoyment to others. We might despatch news from the frontline of events, great and small, to give others thousands of miles away the groundtruth, as we see it, of what is occurring. We might just make a humble record of our lives, in the hope that a great granddaughter will understand better what has gone before, and what yet may be. The democratisation of content creation can only be a powerful force for good. Our own efforts are beautiful and full of meaning. Let's use digital to make more of them, and, in a world packed with distraction, celebrate the act of creation.

Glossary

NB: some of my technical definitions will not satisfy purists. They make do for me. I've also tried to meet the needs of my parents who are totally undigital and observed that there were many terms they were unfamiliar with. The most obvious items I've assumed are understood – like the Internet.

3G – third generation phones, which use a technology for data transfer which is faster than *GPRS*

Amazon – a well known web site that sells books, CDs and lots of other things

Avatar – a symbol or animation that represents a user

Bandwidth – the amount of information that can be squeezed through a communications channel, such as a telephone wire

Blog – is a personal web site featuring thoughts, photos and links to other places on the web – essentially a kind of easy to update public on-line journal

Bluetooth – a technology that allows devices (like phones and PC's) to talk to each other (identify themselves and send and receive content) when they are close (10 metres or so)

Broadband – fast connection to the Internet

Buddy lists – an address book for *Instant Messaging*

Bulletin board – a "place" where users can leave electronic messages for each other and respond to what they see

CCTV – closed circuit TV

CD Rom – a computer CD which stores data

Chat – very similar to *Instant Messaging*

Convergence – a term used to describe the coming together of computing, TV and telephony

Cyberspace – a term used to give a spatial sense to the data networks, usually it means the Internet

DAB – digital radio i.e.: not FM or MW (you need a new kind of radio to receive it)

eBay – the leading Internet auction site where people trade with each other

e-mail – the digital equivalent of the post, through the Internet

Extranet – like an *Intranet* but with restricted access for selected outsiders

Forums – an on-line space where users discuss issues

Friends Reunited – a website which allows ex schoolfriends and work colleagues to find each other

Google – the leading Internet search engine (i.e.: it finds resources such as web sites for users who type in a query)

GPRS – a technology which carries data to and from phones

GPS – global positioning system: it uses satellites to establish very accurate co-ordinates for device fitted with it

GSM – the predominant global mobile phone network standard

HTML – the language that many web pages are written in

Hyperspace – a term used interchangeably with *Cyberspace*

Inbox – the place your *e-mails* arrive

Instant Messaging – a form of immediate text chatting done through the Internet, where more than two users can engage in a conversation

Interactive – used usually to describe a medium where the user can make lots of choices and talk back

Intranet – web based internal information networks for organizations which outsiders cannot look at

IP – either Internet protocol – a communications language computers use, or intellectual property, depending on the context

iPod – the portable digital music player from Apple

IT – information technology

Knowledge management – the discipline that seeks to understand how organizations can make best use of the knowledge stored in their people and systems

LCD – liquid crystal display, a kind of screen for displaying data (usually pictures, words, information)

Mail browser – the software that allows you to send and receive *e-mail* on your PC

MMS – a picture messaging system on mobile phones

MP3 – a standard digital recording format for music

Muds and moos – early forms of community on the Internet

P2P – Internet services which allow users to share files on their computers

Personal organizer – a handheld digital diary, address book and notebook

Portal – a gateway, usually used to mean somewhere people start in order to find other content

PVR – a device under your telly which records programmes to a hard drive, not a tape and allows a range of other things to be done – they can be programmed to recognize similar programmes to your favourites and record them

Real Time – as it happens, not delayed

RFID – radio frequency identification. RFID tags or chips, some no bigger than a grain of rice, allow remote tracking of anything that they are attached to

Ringtone – the calling noise made by a mobile phone, now often in mimicry of a well known piece of music

Search engine – *Google* is the best known of these

Sim cards – the little card which tells your mobile which network provides you with a service, and what your phone number is (it carries other data too)

SMS – the text messaging system that allows mobile users to send and receive small messages of no more than 160 characters, typed in using the phone's keypad

Spam – *e-mail and text messages* you do not want to receive/did not ask for, usually commercial

---

TCP/IP – the technical language that allows computers to recognize and talk to each other over the Internet

Text message – another term for *SMS*

Text news alerts – an *SMS* with a news item sent to your mobile phone

TiVO – a well known brand of *PVR*

URL – a web site address

Video conferencing – using video to connect up people in separate places

Viral marketing – a form of marketing that hopes people will spread the marketing message themselves, like measles

Virtual Reality – something that does not exist in the physical world of things you and I can touch, but is only accessible through a digital medium such as a PC connected to the Internet

WAP – a protocol that allows you to look at the Internet on your phone

WAP Push – a form of message sent to your mobile, that might contain the address of a *WAP* site (a web site specially made for phones)

Web browser – the software that finds and displays web pages for you on the PC screen

Web Cam – a camera linked to a Web page displaying constantly updated pictures

WiFi – wireless broadband (i.e.: lots of fast connection to the Internet without plugging anything in)

Windows – the software that provides the operating interface on your PC